# THE CHANGING FACE OF MUSIC

*BY THE SAME AUTHOR:*

SOUNDS AND SIGNS
(OUP, 1974)

PLAYING THE CELLO
(with Anna Shuttleworth)
(Novello, 1970)

162

CALGARY PUBLIC LIBRARY

780.03 COL  11/2010
Cole, Hugo.
The changing face of music
79062630

ARTS & REC.

# THE CHANGING FACE
# OF MUSIC

by

## HUGO COLE

LONDON
VICTOR GOLLANCZ LTD
1978

© Hugo Cole 1978

ISBN 0 575 02496 8

Printed in Great Britain at
The Camelot Press Ltd, Southampton

DEDICATED TO
MY FRIENDS PICTURED WITHIN

## CONTENTS

|     | Preface                                            | 9   |
|-----|----------------------------------------------------|-----|
|     | Acknowledgements                                   | 12  |
| I   | THE SLOPING PLAYGROUND                             | 13  |
| II  | THE WAY WE LIVE NOW                                | 20  |
|     | Composers in the throw-away age                    | 23  |
|     | Amateurs and professionals                         | 29  |
|     | Rewards and penalties of orchestral life           | 34  |
|     | Soloists and conductors                            | 39  |
|     | The public face of music                           | 46  |
|     | The State steps in                                 | 50  |
| III | MUSIC AND TECHNOLOGY                               | 60  |
|     | Medium in search of a character                    | 61  |
|     | Imperfect, pluperfect: two faces of music          | 65  |
|     | Influences and cross-influences                    | 72  |
|     | New sounds                                         | 79  |
|     | Death of silence                                   | 83  |
| IV  | WORLDS APART                                       | 89  |
|     | Church music                                       | 90  |
|     | Brass bands                                        | 96  |
|     | Light music in decline                             | 101 |
|     | Avant-garde                                        | 104 |
| V   | THE PAST THROUGH THE EARS OF THE PRESENT           | 110 |
|     | Early music                                        | 110 |
|     | Authenticity                                       | 113 |
|     | Cult of the masterpiece                            | 118 |

| VI | QUESTIONS OF COMMUNICATION | 122 |
|---|---|---|
|  | Power of the word | 125 |
|  | End of the line | 133 |
| VII | SPIRIT OF THE AGE | 142 |
|  | Diabolos in Musica | 145 |
|  | Further Reading | 149 |
|  | Select Bibliography | 151 |
|  | Index | 155 |

# PREFACE

THIS BOOK GIVES some account of the present state of music—that is to say, of the organisation and growth of the musical state-within-a-state; of the customs, interrelationships, ideals, preoccupations and prejudices of all whose lives are centred in music: as amateurs or professionals, as composers, performers, entrepreneurs or listeners. It is a book about processes of change; for in the electronic age, nothing remains as it was. Sounds are produced and reproduced in new ways, old communication patterns are superseded, new alliances are formed, old ones are dissolved. The boundaries of the state are enlarged to take in new species of listener and half-listener; we are all faced with new problems and new opportunities—these last sometimes ignored or unrecognised by serious musicians, who are for the most part isolationists, suspicious of any change from without that threatens their independence or freedom of action or that devalues hard-won skills.

This interim report deals mainly with music in England; though I believe that many of my general conclusions would apply as well to other Western countries. I have not attempted to cover every aspect of our musical life, but have tried, by a sampling process, to give a balanced view of the over-all scene. But I have written about certain sorts of functional and popular music which are ignored by most writers on (serious) music, or which are mentioned only in superior or dismissive ways. Church music, band music, light music and background music are not often 'significant' or 'influential' in having any direct effect on the language or idiom of serious music; but sometimes anti-influence counts for as much as direct influence. Popular music moves into an area and serious music moves out. Certain styles and certain instruments or instrumental combinations are rendered *impossible* by popular use. The difficulty and abstruseness of much contemporary art-music reflect directly the banality and instant availability of commercial music. I also believe that many of these musics are worth investigating for their own sakes, and that it is just as important for the highbrow to understand why the lowbrow enjoys sentimental ballads, brass bands, pop and rock, as it is for the lowbrow to understand why the highbrow enjoys Bach, Beethoven or Boulez.

There are obvious dangers in turning attention away from *music itself* to write of performers who interpret and misinterpret; of listeners who understand and misunderstand; of the users and misusers who come and go in every generation and of the mysterious ebbing and flowing of taste and opinion which clouds and distorts our view of *music itself*. Yet there are dangers too in the attitudes of purists who deal only with ideal ways of performing and understanding music, and of analysts who, blinded by staring too long at the sun, retreat into the inner recesses of their own minds. Unless we take into account real-life uses of music, and the ways in which it acts on our minds and emotions in everyday life, we can hardly be said to understand music at all. Real uses may be far removed from ideal uses. Beethoven would no doubt have been astonished to hear his works used as vehicles for star conductors and virtuoso orchestras; as performance material at competition festivals; arranged for steel bands; broadcast in banks or used as background music for washing up to. Yet all such uses lead to contacts, of a sort, with greatness.

In writing about the contexts of music, I do not consider that I am writing of background phenomena. The linguist Urban once wrote that 'the meaning of the word does not exist apart from its context' and I would similarly maintain that 'the meaning of music does not exist apart from its context', and that the study of contexts (fascinating for its own sake) becomes an urgent necessity in times of rapid change. In an age of stability, the context can be taken for granted. Historians can write about music in ideal, abstract terms, trace lines of influence, pigeonhole species of composer, draw up evolutionary trees to explain how new styles and idioms are born, secure in the knowledge that there is a compact body of music-lovers who share assumptions as to the nature and purpose of music and have a common understanding of each man's place in the order of things. Today, there is no common understanding, few shared assumptions, and no one vantage-point from which to view the scene. That is why, if we want to understand fully the meaning of music today and the place which it occupies in real life— in England, in the 1970s—we have to imitate Alice, who found that she could never reach the looking-glass house by walking straight towards it. Instead, she had to walk in the opposite direction, and soon found herself on the doorstep. We have to turn away from the sun, and catch its beams reflected from a thousand surfaces and at a thousand curious angles.

In describing, and to the best of my powers accounting for, some of the changes that have lately come upon us, I have done my best to avoid tendentious personal judgements and prophetic utterances. But anyone living in the midst of things must have his own hunches about the way things are likely to go, and about the way he would like them to go. I end this preface by voicing three of my own special hopes for the future; optimistically upgrading them into *beliefs*:

I believe in the possibility of closer collaborations, not only between composers and performers, but between teams of composers (as in the popular music world) and between composers and technologists; in which the technologists might sometimes be allowed the last word.

I foresee that many of the most interesting developments of the future will be initiated from below, from areas of irresponsible play.

I believe that the attitudes and needs of the new listeners of the electronic age must come, in time, to affect the character of *music itself*.

*Hammersmith*
*25 February 1978*

# ACKNOWLEDGEMENTS

A few phrases, sentences or paragraphs in this book have appeared in criticisms and articles written for the *Guardian*, *Country Life*, *The Listener*, *Tempo* or *Composer*. I would like to thank Peter Williams, of the British Muzak Corporation, for much useful information on the workings of the background music industry. I am grateful to Catharine Carver of Gollancz for many suggestions on presentation which have helped me at a late stage to clarify my own thoughts on several points. And particular thanks to Livia Gollancz, for never-failing support and encouragement over the five years that have passed since this book was first projected.

H. C.

# I

## THE SLOPING PLAYGROUND

THE PLAYGROUND SLOPES gently from one end to the other, and has also a corkscrew tilt so slight that the children only notice it when they begin to play 'the game'. That is, the game which has evolved in the playground, and to which many generations of children have contributed their share.

The game evolves out of its environment. The slope of the ground gives advantages or disadvantages to players in certain positions, and knowledge of the ground dictates the strategy of the game. The ball may bounce back unpredictably from the wire guards over the windows; there is a drain cover in one corner in which the ball may lodge for an extra score. If the ball is hit clean through the hole in the wire netting, the hitter scores 50, but the whole side is 'out'. There was once a grass patch, officially declared out of bounds; but in actual play it is accepted that anyone can go on it as long as the headmaster is out of the way, and the grass has long ago vanished.

But that is the only rule made to be broken. Now that many generations have played the game, its rules have become hallowed by custom and are regarded as sacrosanct. The familiar environment becomes imperceptible and so discountable, and the game takes on an absolute character. The new boy can no more imagine the rules changing than he can imagine the sun standing still. Though the game has grown out of the shape of the playground and the psychological and physical characters of its players, it seems to him that the playground must have been built so that the game could be played, and that it was devised to improve his health and character. The headmaster even implies this in his first address of the term, and has codified the rules, which are issued in cyclostyle to all new boys. Henceforward, the rules decide how the game is to be played.

The new boy is not necessarily wrong in thinking that the game may form character and that playgrounds may be built so that the game can be played. Successful games seem not only to attract but to breed distinct species of players. Games may be exported, and the particular room or space where the game was first played will be reproduced in the game's new home (as in the case of fives courts and 'real' tennis courts). English émigrés have hopefully tried to instil English virtues into Africans and Indians by teaching them to play cricket or football.

The longer the game has been played and the more people play it, the harder it becomes to change the rules of play. The rules are formalised and are up on the notice board; changes can only be made as a result of serious thought by serious, responsible people—sports masters, prefects, members of old boys' associations, who will be hottest of all in defence of old traditions. It is easier to invent new traditions (on the lines of 'from Tuesday next it will be a tradition that new boys do not walk on the grass') than to get rid of old ones. So the game in the enclosed community tends to become more select, and more specialised. If it is widely played, it is held in shape by the need to maintain common standards. Equipment becomes standardised, and the use of technical aids is strictly controlled. The use of performance-enhancing drugs is seen as a means of gaining an unfair advantage; Robin Hood is doubly outlawed if he brings along radio-controlled arrows to the archery contest.

As in other human activities, the momentum of the going system is a strong force acting against change. Established players who have learned the rules and built up skills don't want to be put back in the position of beginners. But over and beyond such practical considerations, there is a belief in the *game in itself*. Thanks to the wisdom of our ancestors, a right way of playing has been evolved. The length of a cricket pitch is not a thing we argue about; it is our duty to preserve the rituals and observances of the game in their strict form.

Musicians have little need for playground walls, being for the most part natural isolationists. They go their own way, ignoring as far as they can turmoil and confusion in the world outside. Music offers them models of ideal order; companionship within the ensemble; the chance to be superbly passionate or infinitely rational, without running themselves into the impossible situations that would arise if they followed passion or reason to the exclusion of other ends in their everyday lives.

We have been playing the same absorbing game for so long that it has acquired a momentum which resists all sudden change. Laboriously acquired skills and habits of mind are not quickly abandoned. Familiar notations, established methods of manufacturing instruments and other musical equipment, fix us in our habits of thought and behaviour. Opera directors and concert agents, music-club secretaries, critics and publicity men all play their part in keeping the system going on its set course.

As in the playground, so in music: a period of stability breeds a belief in the game for its own sake. Music's functional origins are forgotten; we become more serious, and become aware of our responsibility to maintain the game in its one true form. The idea of what must not be done becomes as important as the idea of what may be done. Practical rules take on the character of sacred laws, and a curious reversal takes place. Instead of 'music' being the sounds made by live musicians using the means and instruments that come to hand, 'music' is thought of as an ideal essence, whose nature can only be dimly realised in real-life performances. Theorists become as subtle as theologians in discussing the sacred principles of tonality or thematic relationships. The works of composers of the past, practical men who turned out symphonies and concertos to meet day-to-day needs, are studied as if they were holy runes, riddles to which the one true answer must be found.

When change threatens, those of the true faith join together to defend the purity of the musical game against the environment. Against commercialism; against contamination by contact with lower cultures. Even those who rebel against the stiff conventions of the great games insist that if change comes, change must be dictated from within the system, not arbitrarily imposed from without.

Patterns of play in the recognised official games have been fixed and codified; the feats of great players of past and present have been endlessly written about and discussed; the aesthetic, philosophical, tactical and political significance of every move explained by men of wit and learning. But we can still discover, at the lower end of the playground, many varieties of free, irresponsible play and unofficial games which go unrecorded and almost unnoticed by the chroniclers of the great games. The unofficial singing, skipping and dancing games played by children often have a long unwritten history; they are varied and improved on, brought up to date. They are, so to speak, the folk music of the playground, for long disregarded by those in authority and only lately thought worthy of attention by sociologists. Occasionally, a craze for some offbeat activity sweeps through the community; children rediscover yo-yos or discover skateboards, and in a short time develop astonishing new skills. The authorities tolerantly ignore these mushroom activities. They feel confident that the children who play them will grow up to join in the great games, and will forget about the avant-garde indiscretions of their youth; and generally they are justified. Passionate skateboarders turn into equally passionate footballers; and (in England at least) daring avant-garde composers generally end up as pillars of the establishment.

But there is no question of the great games being in any way affected or influenced by change from below; and some games are tabu at all times, anywhere in the playground. The school community is an élite community, and for any member of the group to play certain sorts of common street games—generally regarded as debased versions of the true games played within the playground—would be a sort of treason, a moral and aesthetic crime. Street music—popular music—music of the *lumpenkultur* cannot decently be mentioned in polite society or in the older sort of dictionary of music.

Musical games change their nature slowly, if at all, in response to dramatic and violent changes in the world without. As Tovey wrote: 'The musical composer is the most detached of artists. For him the time is either out of joint or irrelevant'; the same is broadly true of every committed musician. He has a remarkable ability to insulate himself against change. Like a juggler on a storm-tossed ship, he will contort himself desperately and wonderfully in his efforts to preserve equilibrium. Furthermore, in times of disruption, the public loses what appetite it ever had for music that breathes the spirit of revolution. Music is then valued (if it is valued at all) as a symbol of stability, order, purposeful activity and togetherness. The music of revolution is popular and traditional; designed, as Shostakovich once said, 'to cement the ranks of the people and lead them onwards'. Composers from the world of high art may affirm their patriotism or solidarity with the masses by writing choruses and victory marches; but the *great* music of war and

revolution is arbitrarily selected by the people themselves.*
Only on the rarest occasions does a serious composer become
actively involved, in a musical capacity, in world events. The
figure of Ethel Smyth, conducting her specially-composed
'Suffragettes' March' with a toothbrush from the window of
Holloway gaol, is, from the historical viewpoint, a freakish
exception to the normal rules.

Nevertheless, musical games change surreptitiously, even
when the explicit rules suffer no change. Chamber music
designed for the private enjoyment of performers, with perhaps
a few noble eavesdroppers listening in, is now performed in
great concert halls for the benefit of passive audiences. Conversely, 'public' music of earlier times, such as the dance music
and municipal 'tower music' of the sixteenth and seventeenth
centuries, is adopted by amateur recorder and crumhorn
players for domestic use. The revival of early music is undertaken as an exercise in conservation and detection. Specialists
may respond to the music for its own sake; but they are also
fascinated by the detective problems involved and may even
value the music as potential thesis material. The puzzles and
conundrums that have to be solved may thus become a very
important part of the musical game. A parallel situation exists
in the world of competition festivals. Brass bandsmen competing
for a trophy are playing a double game. A nice clean piece of
phrasing in the *Egmont* Overture does honour to Beethoven and
simultaneously wins valuable points for the band.

Great changes take place when games are professionalised,
and are played to entertain spectators rather than for the
players' own satisfaction. Even when the rules do not change,
the spirit of the game changes; as Huizinga wrote, 'The spirit
of professionalism is no longer the true play spirit; it is lacking
in spontaneity and carelessness.' Football becomes a defensive
game where players are determined *not to lose*; the casual
amicable amateur spirit evaporates and the players bend the
rules in ways amateurs would consider unsportsmanlike,
indulging in time-wasting, deliberate tackling, or intimidation.
Professional musicians are lucky if they are not expected to

---

* The French populace selected, surprisingly, the rambling 'Marseillaise',
composed or adapted by a captain of engineers. The heroes of the Risorgimento selected Verdi's opera choruses. In the Second World War, soldiers
of both sides selected for their theme song the almost unknown cabaret song
'Lili Marlene'.

behave *unmusically*: over-rehearsing in search of the sort of ultra-perfection on which recording contracts depend; or putting on exhibition games in which (as in the all-in wrestling match) they feign and exaggerate joy and agony, chloroforming their artistic consciences as they play, for money, music they would never play for love.

It is, none the less, amazing how far musical games have held their shape. Even during the great restructuring of society that followed the Industrial Revolution, musicians contrived for the most part to keep music and politics in separate compartments and to ignore the social changes that were taking place around them. The great revolutionaries of the age, from Beethoven to Schoenberg, were traditionalists in their determination to preserve the structure and integrity of the musical state-within-a-state. And this state proved itself well able to resist or absorb change. The triangular relationship between composer, performer and listener remained very much what it had been in the days of courtly and aristocratic patronage. Public concerts continued, till the end of the century and beyond, to be modelled on eighteenth-century principles. Technological developments which threatened to bring changes in the established way of life were ignored or treated with extreme caution. Only those in the areas of irresponsible play at the lower end of the playground—popular musicians, bandsmen and music-hall artists—experimented with new types of ensemble, new instruments, and new techniques, uninhibited by any sacred traditions. Serious musicians perpetuate the myth that significant changes are never brought about from below; yet it was the 'flashy' violin virtuosi of the eighteenth and nineteenth centuries who introduced *sautillé* bowings and artificial harmonics, the bandsmen who welcomed valved brass and saxophones, the theatre musicians and jazz players of the inter-war years who took up tuned and exotic percussion and enriched the vocabulary with split and bent notes, long before the serious artists cautiously and deliberately yielded ground and allowed new instruments and new techniques into the system.

But in the last fifty years, the position has changed, not as a result of world wars or social revolution, but because technology, in alliance with commercialism, has forced the pace. Whether the musician is the willing or unwilling ally of the technologist and the businessman is an academic question;

for (in the Western world) he has never had the possibility of choice. The musician can no longer pretend to be sole master in his own house. The invention of the thermionic valve, microphone, tape and cassette recorder, photo-copying machines, and the high-pressure promotional methods that have been used to develop their use have changed the character of musical society and brought about a new balance of power.

Musicians of the 1900s could no more have predicted these new developments than a biologist could predict the occurrence of a chance mutation in some plant or animal which would place the entire species in a new relationship to its environment, possibly enabling it to expand into new habitats, taking a new hold on life; possibly working in exactly the opposite direction, spelling extinction for the mutant species. But in music, the development of electronic technologies spells a new beginning rather than an end. They have brought into being huge new audiences for every sort of music (including serious music); new types of performers with radically changed attitudes; new relationships between composers, performers and listeners; new types of listeners; new alignments and groupings between professionals and amateurs; an expanded and sophisticated industry of promotion and exploitation which threatens to take over and run the whole show. These changes were not willed by us; they happened *to* us.

The sloping playground has flattened; the wall from which the ball has bounced back for so many generations has deformed itself into a new shape, so that no one can foretell in which direction the ball will return. Gangs of strangers appear through new gaps in the wall, anxious to play the game their own way, ignorant of the unwritten traditions that have governed the conduct of the inmates for as long as man can remember. Yet even now, the musician refuses to be hustled into the future. Should we admire him for his self-sufficiency, and applaud his determination to keep alive the spark of humanity in a soulless world of technology and materialism? Or should we blame him for his obstinacy in refusing to take account of new opportunities, or to come to terms with the potential listeners of the future? For the moment, moral judgements are best put aside. The practical and immediate need is to understand what is happening to music and why it is happening, and to interpret the signs and omens that indicate what is likely to happen in the years ahead.

## II

## THE WAY WE LIVE NOW

Most men and women who practise a recognised trade or profession, and particularly one that has been known to many ages and cultures, exist for the world and for themselves on several levels. No man escapes from his archetypal image—as the musician discovers when he tries to insure a hired car. If he puts himself down as 'musician' the rate goes soaring—assuming that the hirers will insure him at all. Better to sign on as teacher, or even as journalist. The archetypal musician is unworldly, unpractical, unable to manage money; long-haired in a short-haired age, bearded in a clean-shaven age; more likely than most men to run off with his neighbour's wife; generally against authority.

I'm aware, as I fill in the insurance form, that I don't match up too well to the popular idea of what a musician should be. This is partly because 'musician' means something very different to me and to the insurance company. For the company, the musician to be reckoned with is the pop musician, dashing off in his van to the next gig. It's easy to forget that I belong to the small sub-class, 'serious musician'. But even among lovers of serious music, the image of the wild, intractable musician—an amalgam of Beethoven, Liszt, Wagner and Mahler—still persists. He is there in the American paperback *Philharmonic*, by Herbert Russcol and Margalit Banai, as he was in Margaret Kennedy's *The Constant Nymph* and in Mürger's *Scènes de la vie de bohème*. The few who have written with inside knowledge and understanding of (serious) musicians, including George Eliot, William de Morgan, Aldous Huxley and Anthony Powell, still preserve a little of the archetype in their portraits. The archetypal character is not pure myth—for every true musician, whether he is composer, performer or listener, is liable to be possessed by the powers of music, which may render him not so much anti-social as a-social. The musician may give a credible imitation of a respectable, conforming citizen; but there are times when, possessed by dark, unknowable forces, he declares his independence and separation from the everyday world of practical affairs. It is these dark forces that the naïve observer builds into his picture —caricatured, exaggerated, or oversimplified perhaps; but corresponding to basic truths which cannot be ignored.

Musicians act out the parts assigned to them by society (and which are also theirs by natural right) with varying degrees of conviction. The flamboyant dress and behaviour of some star performers, on and off platform, may be part of an act that has been developed with half an eye on the public response; but this does not necessarily imply insincerity. The hysterical fits of patients under observation by doctors and scientists can be prolonged by the flattering attention of the experts, but are not for that reason less genuine. Pop singers and star conductors (the only musicians, as Bernstein once said, paid to have epileptic fits in public) function on two levels; they provide the necessary image of the archetypal musician, but may also be technically fully equipped to carry out the job required of them. In the same way, a popular broadcaster on gardening like the late Fred Streeter played the part of crusty old gardener to perfection, and was no doubt conscious of his success in the role. But he was a real gardener too.

In the anti-romantic 1920s, many serious musicians rejected the image assigned to them. Even concert pianists followed Paderewski in cultivating a noble stillness on the platform. The alternative image of composer or performer as an alert, watchful technician, plotting his course as carefully and responsibly as the pilot of an aeroplane, gained favour. Today, if we are to judge from publicity handouts and agency portraits, both images are current. Pictures of Bernstein, Tortelier or Mick Jagger tell us that there is a wild man under the skin of the performer; but there is also attraction and a sort of romance in views of Haitink or Solti, Brendel or Henze, surrounded by dials at the playback of their latest record, their brows furrowed with concentration and anxiety. A few, like Stockhausen, are shown in both rôles; perhaps the ideal musician of our day is visionary and technician simultaneously?

In nineteenth- and early twentieth-century England, the archetypal musician was a foreigner, allowed many eccentricities which would have been frowned on in true Englishmen. It is significant that we continued to talk of *artistes* and *quartettes* and *maestri* until well into the present century. Native English musicians have generally kept to an English reserve in dress and manners. Composers of the past have not needed to act the parts of English gentlemen, since many of them *were* of gentlemanly origin, and those who were not often came to conform to the standards of those who were. Elgar, in adopting the style and manners of a country gentleman, was perhaps aligning himself, consciously or unconsciously, with the English composers of his day, as Sullivan had done before. Today, most serious musicians seem anxious to merge with the society of which they are part rather than to declare themselves—by dress, behaviour, or by congregating in small social groups. How many English composers retreat to remote parts of the land to work out their destinies in solitude! English orchestral players, even when in everyday dress at rehearsal, present such a thoroughly normal and respectable appearance that one suspects they are adopting a disguise to conceal the fact that they are not as other men.

Professionals and amateurs alike tend to keep their artistic and their everyday characters separate to a greater degree than other creative or re-creative artists. Music students involve themselves less in politics, the sister arts, or sociability for its own sake than art students or acting students. The problem for their teachers is often not to encourage them to concentrate on their work but to encourage them to take a look at the world around them. We expect poets, painters and authors to show some correlation between their artistic and their worldly lives (so that their letters and biographies generally throw some light on their creative activities), but it is often hard to discern any connection at all between a composer's work and his manner of life. The performer who excels in romantic, sensuous interpretations may be the most dry and matter-of-fact of men; the intellectual musician may be a sensualist in everyday life.

Musicians tend to retreat into their own ideal world of sound; it seems that ability to cope with all the problems that arise within that world is often paid for by inability to cope with the problems of the real world—the lives of Mozart, Beethoven, Schubert, Wagner and Wolf support such a view. The public would like to tie each composer and his works up together in a neat parcel, and to be told about his philosophy of life to help them with the always difficult task of getting to know the music. But in fact works, lives and philosophies often seem to be bundled together in almost random parcels; while composers and performers, aware that they have said what they had to say in the one medium they can use with mastery, maintain a protective silence. The musician—whether he's a pop guitarist, a back-desk second violin, or an avant-garde intellectual—deals in dark and sacred matters, and must preserve his holiness intact.

*Composers in the throw-away age*
The number of serious composers in England who earn their living from composition is small—probably between 5 and 20—but at least, over the last 50 years, their lot has steadily improved. Since the establishment of performance right and the spread of radio, film, recording and television, they have discovered many new sources of income, which have more than made up to them for the decline in sales of sheet music. A few have grown rich on royalties derived from much-performed works. Part-time composers find it easier than ever before to get comparatively congenial musical jobs in education, broadcasting corporations or musical administration.

Yet when we consider that there are about 400 composers in the Composers' Guild of Great Britain—and perhaps half as many again outside the Guild—it becomes clear that (financially speaking) composing can hardly be considered as a 'profession' at all. Statistics based on a questionnaire sample of 575 composers showed median annual earnings (in 1972) amounting to only £357 a year (£185 for 'serious' composers). Nearly all relied on other sources for the greater part of their earnings; more than half of those sampled earned less than 20 per cent of their total income from composition. For most, by far the greater part of their income from composition comes from performing fees. Yet Performing Right Society figures of distribution for 1976 showed that 79 per cent of their membership received less than £250 a year from performing rights; only 10 per cent over £1,000.

The popular idea that composers live with their heads in the clouds, forget to change their socks, and never know how much money they have in the bank is unfounded. No one who can master the complex timetable of a contemporary score or lay out a chord sequence so that it shall be playable in double and treble stopping on a violin could be called impractical. They think and care no more and no less about money than other people. Some, like Busoni and Schoenberg, have felt that any mention of money in connection with music was demeaning.

Others, from Beethoven to Stravinsky, have been keen if not always successful businessmen. (Strauss, to do him justice, seems to have been more interested in success than in money.) The majority recognise, realistically, that they are never likely to earn much from composition anyhow, and that the big prizes will be awarded as in a lottery. It is not so much that there is a negative correlation between the artistic worth of music and material reward, as that there is no apparent connection at all.

Virgil Thomson, nevertheless, has maintained that there is a close connection between income source and musical style—those who held non-musical jobs remained naïve; those with unearned income wrote charming music without emphasis and so on. In discreet England, where we rarely discuss our income-sources or advertise them in our living style, it is not easy to arrive at the true facts. But social background seems to influence style more than income-source. The music of our most distinguished gentleman composers (Parry, Vaughan Williams, Bliss among them) has been plain and direct in manner, as though they were conscious of the obligation to avoid superior attitudes, and to throw their minds open to the public as they might have thrown open their parks or country houses.

There are, I think, several reasons why composers, nominally the aristocrats and dictators of the musical world, are paid (on average) so much less than performers, teachers, administrators or conductors. First and most obviously, because the harvest can only be gathered slowly as performances mount up—the composer of a new work is in the position of a nurseryman selling untested seeds; no one (least of all those who organise prize competitions) has yet devised a way of sorting out the worthwhile (financially or artistically) from the worthless. Patrons and publishers will support a few chosen composers according to their hunch—but it often seems they might almost as well have drawn the names out of a hat.

Secondly, because the profession is overcrowded. In any age, there have always been fewer vacancies for the post of 'successful composer' than applicants. But in the past, the composer was only in competition with his contemporaries. Today, he is also in competition with Bach, Beethoven and Brahms; he is in the position of a good conversationalist arriving at a party to find Milton, Shakespeare, Hazlitt and Carlyle already holding the floor. Certainly there are more parties going; but at most of them, the contemporary composer feels dismally that, if he is listened to at all, he is listened to perfunctorily, and out of politeness. The composer is dispensable, and for this reason his work is valued low.

Thirdly, because the composer is really paid not in money (welcome though money may be to him) so much as in job-satisfaction and prestige. Most people consider that in job-satisfaction they do pretty well. If they did not love their job they would not (considering the financial disadvantages) be in the job at all.

In status, the composer heads his profession. Every musician who has committed notes to paper would prefer to be thought of as a composer rather than in any other role. When an illustrious broadcaster who also does some conducting and composition is introduced on the radio, he is announced as 'composer, conductor and teacher'—reflecting the order in which those occupations are valued. 'Composer' is often a courtesy title, indicating that a musician would like to be a composer; which accounts for the presence of many in the guilds and composers' associations at the bottom end of the earnings tables. Who would not choose to be of that select company—in which it is, after all, no disgrace to be outshone by masters of past ages?

Composers are often congratulated on their wonderful good luck in being able to exercise their function: 'it must be the most marvellous thing to hear the sounds you have thought of in your head', people say—and so, of course, even for composers of modest occasional works, it often is.

Yet composers as a class are not particularly contented people. They may have resigned themselves to living thriftily, while others with half their talent grow affluent. But almost all want the approval of the society they live in; approval which seems to be withheld when society does not even grant them a living wage. The peculiar view of life which lies at the root of their being and accounts for their creative ability—the intransigence that leads them to insist on the validity of their personal vision, and to demand that things should go their way and no other way—unfits them for accepting the judgement of others or fitting comfortably into the social scheme of things. Most have, if not a grudge against society, a certain sadness at heart, because their works—which are their children—are too little noticed, praised, and understood.

Whether or not he is a member of a guild or society, the composer elects himself and remains, in thought, a composer till he dies. Society tolerates him, often by ignoring him, so that he can spend a lifetime believing in himself and a waiting recognition. Ernst Roth's remark* that 'The Composers' Guilds in almost every country recruit their members mainly from the ranks of the disappointed' has more than a grain of truth in it. Vain hopes of success are never knocked on the head. The moderately competent performer who falls below the professional standard of his day is soon informed, cruelly and finally, of his failure. For the composer, there are no measures or checks by which success or failure can be finally assessed. Because there have been so many examples of neglected composers rising to late or posthumous fame, and because the judges have so often proved fallible, the unsuccessful composer continues to hope—there is always tomorrow!

The composer plans for a better future which, in his own heart, he suspects will never materialise. In a musical world which supports itself mainly on the works of dead composers, the living composer is in the position of the descendant of a once-powerful royal family. There were once great kings, and it is fitting and decent that honour should be paid to their descendants, and that the forms and observances which belong to a great country ruled by great kings should be duly observed. And so, lip-service is paid to the living composer. In principle, his word is law, and he alone has the right of command. But the controlling powers are careful that he shall have only the rarest opportunities to exercise his hereditary powers, and do not allow him the means to support himself in his hereditary station.

As the main function of royalty today is to be seen in public, to provide a focus for veneration, to add tone to state occasions, but never to exercise real authority, so the composer is invited to sit on panels, to judge the works of other composers, to talk about composing; but only rarely to exercise his proper function. Those who commission new works often do so for conscience's sake: that is, because we all agree that composers *should* be supported. When a living composer's work does come to performance, it is treated with the same respect as is shown for the works of the greatest masters of the past. In formal relationships, the composer is still honoured—no matter how

* In *The Business of Music* (1969). Other recent musical sources quoted in passing are listed in the Select Bibliography at p. 151.

patently inadequate he may be to his high office, performers still almost walk backwards out of his presence. They will ask his opinion on every point, prepare the first and (probably) the last performance of a new work as solicitously as the warder supervising the condemned man's last breakfast.

Society venerates composers, but can get along without them; pats them on the head, then tells them to run away and play. This does not make for happiness—there is no frustration so great as that of the eager, energetic man or woman with no resistance to work against. No wonder that many composers retreat into despondent silence; or become convinced that the world is in conspiracy against them; or resort to extreme and provocative behaviour, which in turn convinces society that it was quite right to think that new music is impossible, incomprehensible, or an elaborate confidence trick.

The conditions of a throw-away economy are not necessarily unfavourable to the production of first-rate art, as the experience of the past two centuries surely proves. Minor masters are freed from an oppressive load of responsibility which is more than they can reasonably bear. Greater composers would not necessarily benefit from time, solitude, and freedom from external constraints; many of the greatest works of music and art have been produced quickly and without deliberation in response to urgent demands. The conversational freedom and apparent spontaneity of so many classical and early romantic works surely sprang largely from the composing context, in which works were in fact composed freely and spontaneously, without thought of critics, world markets, the trend of opinion in the years to come which would decide whether posterity frowned or smiled.

But today we are generally committed to the idea that good work should *endure*; and are unwilling to accept the possibility that such an idea may be inappropriate to our own age. We live in an uncomfortable period of double standards. There are 'masterpieces' which are supposed to endure for ever; there are 'occasional works', which we all conspire to forget as quickly as possible. It is generally assumed—still—that every serious composer wants to write music that will endure. Hubert Foss's dictum: 'the one serious aim of the composer [is] the aim to gain a permanent place in 50 or 100 years' time alongside those who are now recognised' does not yet sound as absurd as it should.

It is not easy for composers with a sense of history to acclimatise to the world of the '70s; and many believe that they would be betraying the cause of music if they did. They continue to operate on a buyers' market, refusing to acknowledge that the buyers—the public—have different needs from those of their ancestors. They are like fine craftsmen, whose carefully wrought rings and bracelets are worn for an evening and then, 99 times out of 100, discarded. Not for lack of worth, but because we are geared to a throw-away economy, involving the instant rejection of once- or twice-used material.

Yet those who write for future rather than present audiences can still strengthen themselves in the knowledge that they are following in the footsteps of some of the greatest composers of recent times: Busoni, Schoenberg, Varèse, Bartók and Stravinsky—wanderers and exiles, who chose or were forced to function out of context, often writing for ideal, hypothetical audiences, since the known, familiar audiences to which they might have addressed themselves in more stable times did not exist. (Their circumstances curiously foreshadowed those of today's composers writing for the unknown radio and record audience.) Courage, obstinacy and a great deal of self-confidence were needed to maintain integrity and a sense of direction through the upheavals and revolutions, political and musical, of those years; yet the attitudes appropriate in the first half-century are not necessarily appropriate today. Intransigence is not in itself a virtue. *Jam tomorrow* doesn't follow automatically as a result of *no jam today*.

It would be wrong to suggest that all serious composers are frustrated or unable to adapt to the society of which they are a part. Many natural craftsmen find a niche writing for film, television, theatre, or for schools and amateurs. While opportunities in the first three fields are far too few to absorb all the capable craftsman-composers presently at work, there is now a tradition which allows the most skilled and imaginative composers to put their best efforts into music for schoolchildren and amateurs. Grants, scholarships and subsidies help a composer to exist while he is writing, even if they rarely help him to find an audience. Universities' and Arts Associations' 'composer-in-residence' schemes provide a breathing space and a sometimes too sympathetic milieu—it is often doubtful whether the enclosed intellectual atmosphere of the universities brings out the best in any but natural élitists. And of course some are born to be in a minority, and glory in their hopeless role. They may be liberated by neglect to design fantastic and improbable musical structures, like architects who plan imaginary follies which defy the laws of gravity and the properties of common materials. Such composers would not be happy if the public took them to its heart, and certainly would not know how to make the necessary adjustment to real-life relationships. A limited number develop split personalities, successfully writing 'useful' works which they themselves regard as disposable, and 'serious' works, often in quite different styles and idioms, for the hypothetical audiences of the future.

No doubt in every age there has been spectacular waste of talents, and ours may be no worse than most. The rosy image of the contented eighteenth-century composer-craftsman is not reflected in most eighteenth-century musical biographies. Every age has its misfits, its failures, and its non-starters, who leave no record in history; and every age excludes many who are not tuned to its own particular spirit.

*Amateurs and professionals*
The end of Wagner's *Ring* is approaching. The flames have risen up round the dead hero's bier. Brünnhilde casts herself into the fire, the Rhine rises to engulf the palace of the Gibichungs, Valhalla goes up in flames. The redemption motive is heard, for the last time, high on the strings; harp and string arpeggios climb to the last long-held wind chord. At that moment, I happen to look down from the side of the circle into the orchestra pit—and notice that already, while the wind are still holding out their D flat major chord, most of the string players have pulled out their cases and are busily dusting down their instruments. By the time the conductor gets up on stage and makes his graceful handwave in the direction of the orchestra pit, only the harpists and timpanist will be left, tenderly putting their instruments to bed for the night.

That is professionalism, or one aspect of it that upsets the amateur. How can those hard-bitten men and women be thinking of the last train home, when the rest of us are returning, slowly and unwillingly, from Wagner's extraordinary world, where heroes and gods are transfigured through the power of music? But look at it another way. Do you expect the driver of the coach negotiating hairpin bends on the mountain road to appreciate the scenery? Playing a five-and-a-half-hour Wagner opera is an exhausting, demanding, responsible job, in which nearly all attention goes to doing things the right way, at the right time. Even so, there are players whose eyes fill with tears at the end of *Bohème*: but the overriding need of the professional is to function efficiently. And efficiency means that energies must be conserved, the standard maintained day after day, as though every performance was an audition. That is one reason why he needs to catch the last train home.

The accusation that professionals (and particularly orchestral musicians) are money-minded is at the root of the amateurs' suspicion of the professional; and it would be absurd to deny it. Of course they are money-minded; their livelihood depends on music, as that of the composer does not. They have their human responsibilities, and commitment to their art inevitably stops short of sacrificing security, marriage, or even the Renault or Volvo, to an ideal. It is generally agreed that there is no point in composers discussing the worth of their work in money—there is no correlation between its value and their earnings. But performers can draw up sensible equations relating rates of pay and value of work done, the rate being governed by technical and interpretive skills; ability to work with other people; scarcity value; and (for principals) an element of danger-money.

Because the demarcation line between professionals and amateurs is not too clearly drawn, professionals sometimes tend to be aggressive in self-defence. They will emphasise—and sometimes convince themselves—that they are only in the game for the money, thus avoiding the embarrassment of being importuned to play in charity concerts or lead amateur quartets for the fun of it. But every good orchestral player gets a certain satisfaction from his work, and most enjoy the prestige that always attaches to the public performer—even if he is one of a hundred. His satisfaction cannot be assessed in purely musical terms. The communal feeling within the group may be as important to him as the music itself; while in every orchestra you will find natural craftsmen whose main pleasure comes from the exercising of their skills (you will find such natural craftsmen also among joiners, printers, potters and glass-blowers). Prestige is an important factor which keeps many players in the symphony orchestras, even though they might be earning more in the sessions world. (But it would be a mistake to admire symphony players too much because they don't spend their time recording highly paid television jingles. It is only a very few symphony orchestra players who could stand the strain of sessions life, which demands extreme quickness of reaction, ability to slip in and out of any style and idiom at a minute's notice, and to perform always up to the highest standard under conditions of extreme stress.)

Professional motives, then, are always mixed. Love of money, love of music, the need for recognition and security, are tangled up together in a skein which can never be completely unravelled. Yet whether professionals are content or restive, involved or indifferent (and whether indifference is assumed or genuine) the fact remains that they are committed; they have put all their stakes on one card. They belong to music, and music belongs to them, as it can never belong to the amateur.

For the professional, when he is in a sour mood, 'amateur' means the pianist next door who after six months is still playing the first Chopin Prelude at half speed, with involuntary ritardandos whenever the little finger of the left hand has to seek out the lower bass-notes and with the same agonising suspense over the so-often overlooked F sharp in the sixth bar. 'Amateur' means the conductor who talks for half an hour about Beethoven's secret thoughts and cannot bring the orchestra in on a down-beat; or the violinist who smilingly forgets his mute. The amateur never gets better and does not want to get better; he has a passion for performing in public; he is too serious about himself, and too casual about his art. The amateur's best will never be good enough for the professional—for though standards have risen so that the best amateur orchestras of today are no worse than many professional orchestras of thirty years back, professional standards have also risen so that the sound of approximately-in-tune amateur playing is as painful as ever to finely tuned professional ears. The amateur has time and enthusiasm on his side, and will sometimes perform music which no commercially aligned group could undertake. But gratitude to the university societies which put on obscure nineteenth-century operas is tempered with dismay when singers can only sketch in their parts and when strings cannot get near the notes. Composers who are delighted when amateurs decide to perform their works are a little less delighted when they find the performers making do with less rehearsal than any professional group would allow, totally failing to appreciate the difference between their own enthusiastic performances and those of professionals.

Yet if I had to choose between expertise without enthusiasm —the dead performances of bored professionals—and enthusiasm without expertise, I would find it hard to come to a choice. Luckily, the need to make such decisions rarely arises. Most professionals retain some love of music; many amateurs are reasonably skilled and conscientious.

In fact, we have most of us been amateurs before we became professionals. There used to be professional musical families, as there still are circus families, in which the children were brought up almost from birth to carry on the hereditary trade. But today most performers serve their apprenticeship in school orchestras, youth orchestras, or at the universities before they reach the conservatoires. And a good number of professionals later retreat from the monotonous labour of orchestral life to rediscover, in the freer and more adventurous worlds of early music or avant-garde music, some of the enthusiasms lost in the routine of professional life. There is an amateur under the skin of every good professional.

Professionals often prefer to keep their musical life separate from their social life, guarding their leisure jealously. But from another point of view, the amateur's desire to gear music into life reflects earlier, more primitive stages of musical development, when no one would have dreamed of separating music from ritual, work, dance, or other forms of social activity. The amateur uses music as a sort of social cement. Look at the end pages of the local operatic society's programme of *Chu Chin Chow* and you will find notices of picnic outings, fund-raising campaigns, commemorative coffee evenings. Operatic societies, brass bands and choral societies are clubs as well as musical organisations. The act of playing in ensemble can serve as a substitute for conversation for the shy and taciturn; sympathy may be established in a musical exchange between the second violin and cello of a quartet which could have been established in no other way.

Ultra-professional musicians brought up in countries with no amateur tradition have a great scorn of amateurism. 'We must make the texture of our music such that no amateur can lay hands on it,' Busoni wrote to his friend and disciple Bernard van Dieren. But today, even the most fastidious make an exception in favour of the best youth orchestras and university groups. Stravinsky, who never tolerated slapdash playing, was delighted by an *Oedipus Rex* put on by an Indiana agricultural college, and declared that the Eastman School Orchestra played parts of *The Flood* perfectly, giving on a minimum of rehearsal better performances than a renowned professional orchestra could manage after a week of rehearsals. Boulez's memorable performance of *Rite of Spring* with the National Youth Orchestra some years ago showed that it is possible to have the best of both worlds, professional and amateur; to combine technical accomplishment of a high order with a sense of involvement and new discovery which only the young player, coming to a great work for the first time, can convey.

At a less exalted level, I remember a performance of Beethoven's Fifth Symphony by a children's orchestra more moving than any routine Festival Hall version, in spite of technical deficiencies that would have made us rise up and demand our money back at a professional concert, and a school performance of Gluck's *Alceste* that came nearer to the heart of the matter than any I have seen in London. The special quality of such performances springs from long immersion in music, which comes to fill the entire horizon of young performers. What matters, is not that amateur music should be publicly heard, but that it should be played with love and for love. And it does us no harm to be exposed from time to time to the playing of the most unskilled amateurs. It recreates a whole spectrum of possible performance standards—the LSO never sound so good as when we come straight from hearing the junior school orchestra labouring through a Haydn slow movement.

In the nineteenth century, the amateur music movement in England was greatly strengthened by our belief that music was no profession for a respectable Englishman. As a result, our most talented native musicians of the middle and upper classes remained amateurs, unless they took up the one career they could adopt without loss of status: that of organist. So it was that our philistinism created a climate in which the brass bands and great amateur choirs could flourish. Today, they still fill a role which no professional organisations could fill as well. But the social stigma on professionalism has gone. At present, the dividing line between amateurs and professionals is less clearly marked than it is in the other performing arts: drama, dance and circus. In serious and in light music, there is a twilight zone of semi-professionalism, in which union rates are quietly ignored. Professionals and amateurs sing side by side in many of our smaller choirs; though Equity made a move to end the practice in 1977, it seems likely that those involved will go on as before, following the usual English belief that it is all right to sidestep regulations as long as you do it discreetly.

Roberto Gerhard, who was surprised and delighted by the skill and enthusiasm of English amateurs, was also distressed by their conservatism. It is in the nature of amateurs to lag behind the contemporary musicians of the day—technically and emotionally they are unready for Boulez and Birtwistle, and feel quite daring enough if they occasionally put on a work by Britten or Malcolm Arnold. This conservative tendency is reflected in all aspects of our musical life; however advanced we feel ourselves to be, we are still to outsiders a nation of traditionalists. It seems a reasonable deduction that the large proportion of active amateurs in the musical community act as a stabilising—or delaying—force; so that even though they are rarely noticed by historians or critics, it is the amateurs who are largely responsible for the character and colour of the musical life of the nation.

*Rewards and penalties of orchestral life*
Tough, uncommunicative players, who are unwilling to admit they get any satisfaction from music, who regard conductors and orchestral managers with suspicion, who rehearse with one eye on the wristwatch and who would consider it a sign of weakness to take a part home to practise, are still to be met with, though they are fewer and not typical of the profession as a whole. They inherit the pugnacity of those who lived through the depression years of the 1930s and who experienced music's own private slump, which started in 1929 and in a few years put over half the country's professional performers out of work. Before the arrival of the talkies, from three-quarters to four-fifths of the orchestral players in the country had been in the cinemas. In the 1930s, practically all cinema musicians lost their jobs, and the decline of music hall and touring theatre, together with the development of the panatrope, drastically reduced opportunities for work in the theatre pits.

The extent of the change in the nature of the profession since the 1930s can hardly be exaggerated. Before that time, the spectrum of skills among orchestral players was vast—there were semi-skilled theatre players in London and the provinces who viewed the world from the same theatre pit, playing from the same tattered copies, for years on end. There were players in travelling opera companies whose narrow musical horizons never expanded to take in more than the eight or nine operas in the standard repertory. At the other end of the spectrum were those who played in the symphony orchestras; but even the aristocrats of the profession mostly depended for their livelihood on theatre work and on summer seasons with pier or spa bands. Until the BBC formed its own orchestra in 1930, the Bournemouth orchestra was the only full-time symphony orchestra in Britain.

The profession, then, consisted of a very small élite and a very large non-élite. The smallness of the élite is hard to comprehend in the 1970s, when there are dozens of competent applicants for every orchestral vacancy. Bernard Shaw complained, in the 1890s, that by assassinating five or six people, you could have deprived London of every woodwind player of any distinction in the capital. The same statement could almost have been made in the early 1930s. If the Schubert Octet made one of its rare London appearances, it was almost inevitable that Aubrey Brain and Archie Camden were hornist and bassoonist respectively. If the LPO was withdrawn from the ballet pit to take part in a provincial festival, the results were disastrous; it was virtually impossible to assemble a freelance orchestra in London that could cope with *Petrushka* or *Coq d'Or*.

There were, even so, remarkable players about, in the restaurant bands and theatres; as underpaid and unregarded as the starving ploughmen described in Ronald Blythe's *Akenfield*, who ploughed perfect furrows in spite of the malaise of despair. They could be beautiful players—and their work was often the only beauty in their lives. But such men had not the experience or versatility to operate in the wider musical world. The average player was little educated except in his own craft. He was a nomad, of no definable social class—not a white-collar worker and not one of the 'working classes'. He had much in common with the actors of an earlier age, or the circus performers of our own day. Many instrumentalists came from professional families which maintained traditional skills and were wary about passing them on to outsiders; family connections were all-important when it came to entering the profession, and many began deputising in local theatres before they left school.

With the development of radio, recording, and consequent changes in the pattern of demand, the process was already under way in the 1930s that was to lead, in the post-war years, to the virtual restructuring of the orchestral profession. The BBC staff orchestras offered permanent employment, and took in many players straight from the conservatoires. With the new enthusiasm for practical music-making in schools and universities, a new type of orchestral player was coming into the profession, who had never played in restaurant, cinema or bandstand. These younger players sometimes held university degrees (not necessarily in music). They were not aware of any social or psychological feeling of separation from academic or administrative musicians. Orchestral playing has become, since the beginning of the century, one of the respectable arts—like painting, sculpture, woodwork or bookbinding—in which anyone from an earl to a dustman may dabble at evening classes, and in which anyone may find employment without loss of social caste.

The drastic purging of the profession that followed the arrival of the talkies was counterbalanced, in the war years and thereafter, by a great increase in demand for orchestra and chamber music. By the 1950s, London had five symphony orchestras and two opera orchestras in permanent employment and had become one of the world centres for recording, while Glasgow, Birmingham, Manchester, Liverpool and Bournemouth also had their permanent full-time orchestras. Today, the number of professional instrumentalists in the country is quite small. The Musicians' Union has a membership of about a third of the number employed, according to Robert Taylor, in the betting and gambling industries in 1974. Of these only about 5,000 are fully employed—2,000 salaried, the rest as freelance players.

In effect then, there is more room at the top, but a brutal reduction in opportunities for the less talented and resilient—for broadcasting, recording and full-time symphonic work call not only for high technical standards but for ability to withstand stress and great powers of physical endurance. Players of the old school are still around; in military bands, in the few remaining theatre orchestras and in a few provincial orchestras. But orchestral playing has increasingly become a young man's profession. The heavy workload of London orchestras and the taxing travel schedules of provincial orchestras, as perpetually on the move as the Flying Dutchman, impose great strains. In the 1920s, the membership of London's major orchestras changed very slowly. Older players were never anxious to relinquish membership, and the flexible deputy system allowed them to get the main benefits of their jobs while leaving the unrewarding or more exhausting out-of-town dates to their juniors. But broadcasting and recording brought a merciless searchlight to bear on the big orchestras: in the competitive commercial world of recording, managements could no longer allow sentiment or loyalty to influence choice of key players. Star players, like swimming champions, peak and decline ever earlier. Brilliant young players go into positions of responsibility straight from the conservatoires, and only a few have the stamina or will to stay in the forefront for long. The asterisks in the programmes of provincial orchestras denoting twenty years' service become fewer and fewer. The increased number of orchestras enables players to change jobs more easily (one London orchestra worked through nine principal oboes between 1945 and 1960). In the 1970s, the position became a little more stable, probably as a result of the recession which encouraged players who had safe jobs to hold on to them.

On balance, there have been great gains. Orchestral players today have higher status, better work conditions, and a broader outlook in musical matters. There are also some losses. Thirty years ago, people from every sort of background and with every sort of musical experience met in the big orchestras. Today, the social spectrum is narrower. There may have been more freshness and exuberance in the playing of men who spent the week in the theatre pit, for whom the symphony concert was a rare and special occasion. But this is the age of specialism, and we must accept its disadvantages with its advantages.

*Plus ça change* ... in spite of everything, the symphony players remain the most conservative of all musicians. German radio orchestras have gone on strike rather than play avantgarde music; I have heard the brass of a London orchestra interpolate a derisory march-out at a Boulez broadcast (after the red light had gone out). Stockhausen's utopian plans for reform and retraining of symphony orchestras would make no impression at all on most orchestral players, for whom the standard orchestra is still a complete and living organism, which would be disfigured and misrepresented if its constitution was altered, as a human being would be if robbed of an eye, or with an added nose. Perhaps orchestras are all the more conservative now that more adventurous players can find work in the chamber groups. They are guardians of the central and most highly valued of all musical traditions—that of classical symphonic music; and also of some less valued traditions. In spite of the BBC and of Henry Wood's example, the symphony orchestras remain predominantly male, for no reason at all except that men like it that way. Women are accepted in chamber orchestras on equal terms; but in the most lucrative jobs—sessions work, recording orchestras, and in the theatre—the men have jealously preserved their ancient rights to the best jobs.

Orchestral players do not stop grumbling because they are secure. In fact the player who is financially reasonably secure has his mind set free to concern itself with artistic dissatisfactions which (owing to the nature of the job) will never vanish away. Even members of self-governing orchestras work under a dictatorship—the dictatorship of the conductor; and are condemned to an inordinate amount of repetitive work. Beecham once labelled his string players as a body of disappointed soloists. It would be truer to call them disappointed orchestral players—inadequately stimulated by conductors and repertoire, yet sceptical about the value of contemporary music.

For one trouble in taking on a job about which you can, at times, feel genuine enthusiasm is that you can also be driven to despair when music or conductor makes work a drudgery rather than a delight. The power to *turn off*, working to rule with the least possible expenditure of effort and attention (and very little are needed merely to play the notes correctly in familiar repertoire works) is the orchestral player's defence, and may indicate, not so much disillusion with music in general as an excess of musicality of the wrong sort.

The artistic satisfactions are however many—and these too are not easy to put across to those who have experienced music only in a passive, listening role. Hans Keller has suggested that 'it is impossible to be a highly musical and highly accomplished string player and to be happy in an orchestra'; and indeed, orchestral players do hear music in strange and distorted perspective. The truth is, that the orchestral player adapts to his position just as the cathedral organist (who hears his choir a quarter-second after they have begun the note) adapts; or as the singer does, who is not misled by the resonances in his own head to hear the ensemble as a hugely loud solo for himself accompanied by distant voices.

The professional orchestral player, then, may still respond to music as keenly as the amateur; and he can share the secondary pleasures of music-making which play such a large part in the experience of all practical musicians. He can take satisfaction in applying his skills to ever new problems; in sorting out the intricate puzzles of unfamiliar works, producing order out of disorder; in rediscovering familiar works through the intervention of conductors of vision and imagination—even the most jaundiced player will admit that there are still a few such conductors around. Most of all, the player takes satisfaction from being part of, thinking and feeling with, that suprahuman organisation which is the orchestra. It does not at all surprise me that, when Gustav Holst, near the end of his life, listed the four things in life for which he was most grateful, one was: 'having known the impersonality of orchestral playing'.

*Soloists and conductors*

The supply of potential soloists always exceeds the demand. They are in a better position than composers in that (as yet) their services cannot be dispensed with in favour of long-dead predecessors; but competition is fierce, and the passion for communication which drives actors and musicians to seek a soloist's career is often cruelly frustrated. The satisfactions of a soloist's life are great: of being one's own master; involving the personality fully in the service of an adored art; and, at a lower level, of being publicly acclaimed. Soloists are generally ambitious, and ready to suffer for their art. They often prefer to starve in London rather than to prosper in Nottingham or Inverness. But even for the most successful and talented, the dangers and possibilities of unhappiness are great. When so much of the individuality is bound up in the work, it is hardly strange that day-to-day successes and failures should be taken as personal triumphs or tragedies. The identity of a singer or violinist may be crushed or bruised, left tender for years, if he is rejected by audiences or critics. Continued success is always precarious, dependent on robust health,* and as liable to sudden eclipse as that of the athlete.

Unrecognised soloists, like unrecognised composers, may sustain themselves for years on hope. Financing their own recitals with the aim of getting favourable notices to impress the committees of festivals and music clubs; moving from teacher to teacher in the hope of finding the talisman that will open the door to success and recognition; hopefully entering for international competitions. The educational systems of communist countries, which severely limit the possibilities for musical education at higher levels but which do relate intake to demand, may seem to us arbitrary and dictatorial, but are at least effective in reducing the numbers of would-be soloists who live perpetually in a land of unrealistic hopes.

Unless a young performer leaps to fame in one bound by winning a major international competition, he faces many trials of strength and endurance—physical, psychological, musical and social—on the upward path. He will travel to remote parts of the country to perform with under-rehearsed orchestras or on out-of-tune pianos. He learns something about the perishability of musical offerings; not one considerable success is needed, but another, and another, and another . . . before the public and promoters learn to recognise his name, let alone his fame. He learns that his ability to impress committees, to conceal his feelings about inept conductors and accompanists, to smile agreeably when he feels black within, are necessary qualities. His agent may suggest that he change his appearance, his name, his whole personality, to please his hypothetical public. If he pleases them enough, he may suffer Busoni's fate—dispatched like a parcel to towns 'like ingeniously contrived departments of Dante's Hell, where travelling virtuosi who throw away the best part of their lives for fame and money, gnash their teeth in blindness'. Condemned to solitary eminence, he is likely to succumb to disillusion or to the delusions of grandeur that loneliness and the prolonged contemplation of his own gifts induce.

While there is still room for the virtuoso pianist who travels the world with his five or six concertos, and while there are probably still opera houses where the phrase 'stupid as a tenor'

* 'Illness', said Busoni, 'is lack of talent.' A point made even more forcibly by Jack Hylton, who would say to his players: 'Death is the only excuse.'

is repeated with feeling, there is more scope today for intelligent, thoughtful and versatile singers and players; they may not have the hypnotic mass appeal of the great stars, but, thanks to the media of mass communication and comparatively greater ease of travel, they can reach the smaller but more discriminating audiences which have come into existence all over the world. In an age when the public are continually being invited behind the scenes, to meet great performers in radio, TV and press interviews, to watch their rehearsals, home life, masterclasses, or to read their views on music and life, the veil of mystery which once surrounded the celebrity has been torn down. The performances of today's stars, technically faultless, tend to be less mysterious too—there is little room today for the temperamental, unpredictable soloist who experiments in public, using the audience as his guinea-pig.

Only pianists and string players whose lives have centred from earliest years on their relationship with their instruments, stand much hope of reaching the top as soloists today. When one thinks of the man-hours spent by violinists in conservatoires every year mastering the indispensable tricks necessary for successful performance of the great romantic concertos (fingered octaves, double-stopping in artificial harmonics, down-bow slurred staccato . . .), one is amazed, not that there are so few virtuosi with broad musical interests, but that there are any at all. Luckily there are many areas in which the technical barriers are less formidable. Almost as many performers come into early and baroque music from the universities as from the conservatoires. While many excellent scholars are dull performers, and while many of the finest performers use scholarship to justify and make respectable musical acts which are largely intuitive, the breakdown of barriers between academic and practical worlds of music is one of the most cheering features of the present scene.

And in fact, the prospects for soloists of high potential talent of finding a comfortable niche in musical society have improved immensely over the last fifty years. In the days when serious music was restricted to the narrow classical-romantic repertoire and when there was no room for a single permanent quartet or other type of chamber-music ensemble in the land, the highly gifted young musician was in the position of the customer who goes to a shoe shop to find that he has to cram his foot into one of two or three available fittings and styles of shoe. If he was young and pliant, his foot would in time deform to fit the shoe and allow him to lead a moderately comfortable life. If he was not pliant, he would come, like Busoni, to scorn the audiences and the musical society that condemned him to conform to their standards.

But today, even in the small and self-contained world of serious music, the range of choice has widened. Quartet players can devote themselves to their art and hope to find a modest living in universities if not on the concert circuit. Fortunate specialists—on musical glasses, baryton, or cornett—can make a small name in new fields of action. This does not mean that there are fewer frustrated soloists. As the opportunities increase, the dangers of mistaking one's destiny increase too. More and more aspirants are drawn into the game, and the wretchedness of the ambitious soloist who achieves less than he thinks he deserves is as great as ever it was. But the art of music has gained from the influx of new and varied talent. It is not only among the avant-garde that the relationship and balance of power between composers and performers has changed so as to favour the performer. In the nineteenth and early twentieth centuries, far more composers than performers rose to eminence as conductors; today, the position is reversed. Some of the best critical and musicological studies are written by performers. Performers commission works to suit their own requirements, and composers, abandoning the intransigent attitudes of Stravinsky and Schoenberg, are glad to provide material-for-performance as their eighteenth-century predecessors once did. In the worlds of popular music and opera the performer's status has never declined. It may be that historians of the future will regard the period from Beethoven to Boulez—when composers claimed absolute authority and asserted their sole right to dictate the course of musical events—as a period of misrule, when the proper order of things was for some reason temporarily upset. And they will have, somehow, to account for the mysterious rise to notoriety of the conductor—the middleman, who neither creates nor performs, but who is so often thought of as the star of the grandest and most impressive musical occasions.

In a traditional music-hall turn, on which variations are still played, a demure debutante appears dressed up to the nines in voluminous silk, skirts sweeping the ground. After going through the first part of her act in this guise, she makes an about-turn, and we discover her other side, naked except for a few sequins.

The conductor's two aspects are similarly contradictory; but there is the difference that the audience remains unaware of the reverse, flip-side image till the end of the act. To the innocent listener and viewer, he remains the unique being through whom the music flows. He, rather than the composer or the orchestra, is the true creator. But to the orchestra, he is the carver; the man on whom their pay cheques ultimately depend; the one who tells others what to do, but does nothing himself.

'No conductor is a Santa Claus,' one of Ormandy's Philadelphia players said: 'to us, picking your conductor is like picking your poison.' And again: 'A conductor is a good hate-symbol.' The conductor can unify an orchestra after the manner of Saki's Mrs Pentherby, the odious guest who was invited to every house-party so as to inspire a spirit of cameraderie in the other visitors, who could unite in detesting her.

Generally speaking, orchestras will pick on a conductor's weaknesses, taking the good, if they admit it to exist, for granted. They believe—not very reasonably—that 'if a concert goes well the conductor gets the credit; if it goes badly, the orchestra gets the blame'. Orchestral stories often centre on the conductor's passive role. The cymbalist fails to synchronise his clash to the conductor's satisfaction. 'What is easier than to hit two cymbals together at the right time?' the conductor asks rhetorically; the cymbalist replies: 'To conduct a player hitting two cymbals together.'

Composers are hardly more ready to give the conductor the benefit of any doubt; though for obvious reasons they are often circumspect about expressing their opinions. For the conductor is the man with power and with access to the public. But privately, the composer thinks of him as a middleman, and resents the fact that the public regard him as the man who 'makes the music', who is paid more for a night's work than the composer is paid for a year's, and to whom the greatest credit and the largest display type on the posters are given. Famous composers who have nothing to fear will praise individual conductors; but conductors as a species get little mercy. For Ives, they were lily-eared softies with stupid expressions on the backs of their necks. Hindemith saw them as power-mad dictators, Stravinsky as the lapdogs of musical life, or as cosmeticians applying unwanted beauty aids to great music.

It is true that international conductors are mostly specialists in superfine performance; their reputations and recording contracts depend on their ability to polish, perfect and refine, adding the final coat of gloss and brilliance to familiar works.* There is not much inducement for them to risk their reputations on problematical contemporary works, against the scepticism of conservative orchestras and the prejudices of audiences who can rarely appreciate the difficulties they face. And if they are reproached for their conservatism, they can retort with some reason that very few living composers seem to write well for symphony orchestra, and that they are unable to find the works that are worthy of their skills or their public.

Of course there are great conductors—though few as great as the promotions men make them out to be. Yet even critics are sometimes brainwashed into believing that conductors can work miracles. Let a famous conductor appear in the orchestra pit at Covent Garden or Glyndebourne, the next day many reviews will confidently attribute all the musical virtues of the performance to him; overlooking the fact that opera involves the most elaborate network of interacting forces, mechanical hazards, battles of wills, last-minute accidents and adjustments. A conductor, or a principal singer, may upset or inspire the whole company on occasion; but no one without inner knowledge is in a position to say what particular combination of circumstances led to disaster or triumph on a certain evening.

The star conductors, great public figures who lead huge orchestras through familiar works in full view of an admiring public, form only a very small proportion of the whole species. In fact, there are many sub-species, some with specialised characteristics so marked that they are barely recognisable as belonging to the same breed. At the bottom end of the spectrum, there are park band conductors with a good collection of parts and piano-conductor scores and a long list of telephone numbers. No one expects them to be musical geniuses, but they can start and stop an orchestra and hold a tempo. There are the experienced choral conductors, who are rarely successful with professional orchestras—not so often (today) because they are ignorant of orchestral techniques, but because they are not experienced in communicating with highly skilled specialists,

* 'Conductors are never thinking of the public, but rather of what other conductors will think of them when they hear the record. A careless attack ... they detest above all things.' (Fred Gaisberg in *Music on Record*.)

and are accustomed to the teaching situation and the leisurely time-scale of amateur rehearsal. Conductors of amateur orchestras can rarely make the transition to professional music-making for the same reason. Skilled theatre and opera conductors tend to be a race apart—men of astonishingly quick reactions, able to attend to a dozen incoming messages at once, to retrieve desperate situations and weld together disparate elements. Because they cannot successfully transpose themselves into concert-hall keys, they are consistently undervalued. Yet some of the finest opera performances (which often go unnoticed by critics) are directed by staff opera-house conductors, who take over when the world-famous eminence who has presided over the première has flown off to his next engagement in New York or Tokyo.

The qualities needed by a conductor at the upper end of the spectrum are in some ways different from those possessed by the leading conductors of fifty years back. As orchestral players have improved their status and broadened their horizons, and as union representation has strengthened, the authoritarian attitudes that were once common have become less acceptable. Most conductors today, however they may appear to the audience, present themselves to orchestras as fellow-craftsmen. Those who conduct chamber orchestras often function as adjudicators, leaders of discussion, and time-setters on terms of genuine equality. Several successful chamber orchestras are now directed by violinist-leaders in the nineteenth-century manner; but a return to the conductorless ensemble on any large scale seems unlikely—not so much because problems of synchronisation or democratic policy-making are too great, but because players have become so used over the years to working under direction, that they tend to relapse into a neutral style of performance if external stimulus is withdrawn.*

Performers tend to think that conductors are overpaid: in 1976, a rank-and-file orchestral player in London could make £22.50 from a single concert—a star conductor up to £4,000. Part of this 'value' is artificially created by impresarios and

* Given time, however, there seems to be no reason why a conductorless ensemble should not establish itself. *Persimfans*, the conductorless orchestra founded in Russia in 1922, is often referred to as an unsuccessful experiment; but in fact, the orchestra ran for many years, drew large audiences and only ceased to exist as a result of ideological objections (it was suggested that the leader exerted too much influence in what should have been a perfectly democratic organisation).

record companies, who build up a conductor's name because that is the most effective way to sell their music packages. Once a star image has been created, the star becomes unique and irreplaceable in the eyes of the public, and his value soars. But successful symphonic conductors have genuine scarcity value, not so much because their gifts in any one direction are unique, but because the combination of gifts needed—as organisers, as communicators, as psychologists and musicians—is so rarely found all in the same person. Of course a great conductor must have uncommon musicality—but for every great conductor there must be hundreds of obscure musicians with as much insight into the processes of music, with equal gifts of memory and discrimination (somewhere in every orchestra there is a player who can analyse every chord as it sounds, and another with total recall of all the symphonies in the repertory). He must love, but he need not necessarily understand the music he conducts in the sense the composer understood it—sometimes, passionate misunderstanding creates its own sort of authenticity. The conductor proves that he is worth his money when he makes music once more interesting for overworked orchestras, putting back a certain magical unexpectedness into a too familiar situation; or when he tells the audience something new about the music, through the sounds, or by acting out the music so as to turn their attention in certain directions, or simply through the appealing eloquence of his gestures. Leads given may be technically unnecessary, gestures expressive rather than utilitarian. But the conductor is a hypnotist, a magician, a priest conducting strange rites, as well as a musician. He may or may not consciously woo the audience—but he cannot help impressing his own personality on music and on audience. Ultimately, a conductor's worth cannot be measured in terms of the truthfulness or sincerity of his interpretation (in an age of alternative recordings, we have learnt that there are dozens of alternative truths about a great work). It lies in the (potentially fruitful) interaction between his own personality and those of the composer, the performers, and the listeners.

*The public face of music*
The story of amateurs and professionals, of composers, performers and conductors is a story of changing relationships; the character of our society expresses itself in changes of status, and

in our changing assessments and expectations of ourselves and one another. When we reach the entrepreneur, we reach the man who is nothing but a relationship in himself: the go-between who links active partners in music-making. To call someone a middleman is an insult implying that he is a parasite on the body musical, sucking sustenance from it and giving nothing back.

Of all middlemen, the one with the worst reputation is the impresario. He is the subject of many fables. He buys the opera company so that his mistress can play Tosca. He arrives in a new Rolls-Royce and refuses the percussionist porterage charges. He throws a party for the star and cuts the orchestra's salaries. And, of course (the oldest *idée reçue* of them all), 'the impresario decamps with the takings.'

For the archetypal impresario loves money more than music. He is after quick gains. He exploits the musician while his market value is high, drops him when it falls. He has the ear of mysterious powers above, and secures the best hall bookings so that the musician is at his mercy. He interferes with the musician's private life: concert agents still 'advise' their artists on their choice of dress. The musician's view contains an element of caricature. When Busoni wrote of his English agent: 'Everything Mr Powell thought out, undertook and carried through was done tradesman-fashion, and was unworthy, painful and even harmful', he overlooked the possibility that Mr Powell might combine business acumen with genuine love of music. But the biographies of impresarios confirm suspicions that their greatest joys stem from their successes in bargaining, in manipulating, in playing the exciting and dangerous game in which conductors, orchestras and famous soloists are their pawns.

Today's impresarios and agents are mostly of a higher caste than the impresarios known to Busoni. They may themselves have a musical background, and are generally better able to communicate with musicians in a language they can understand. If they still exploit those they hire, they do so politely and with some respect for their musical scruples. There are fewer monopolists in Britain than in America, and they wield less power; for since the BBC and the Arts Council appeared on the scene, the impresarios have often themselves become dependent on the state system and no longer have sole control of opera houses, orchestras or concert halls. 'Big business' is today the villain of the piece. But the target is a broader one, and the record and film companies do not exploit or manipulate musicians in such crude or direct ways as the old impresarios. In fact, they generally pay well and promptly, so that performers, while still objecting in principle to commercialism, find themselves in direct conflict with commercial managements less often than with hard-pressed state-run organisations.

Relations between the composer and his traditional middleman the publisher have also improved, as has the character of the publisher himself. It was nothing, in the eighteenth century, for an unscrupulous publisher to expunge an unsuccessful composer's name from the engraved plates and replace them with that of a famous composer (as Bailleux did, replacing Hofstetter's name by Haydn's, so that poor Hofstetter has ever since lost credit for the op. 3 quartets, including the F major with the famous Serenade). Beethoven's furious correspondences suggest that his publishers treated him as badly as he treated them. But serious-music publishers have long since become respectable members of our musical society. Today, the heads of music-publishing departments are generally musicians themselves, and regard themselves—and are generally regarded—as friends of serious music. Their power and influence has declined with the rise of radio and recording, and the composer does not rely only on his publisher in his efforts to reach the public. In a confused situation where record companies set up publishing companies, publishers set up record companies, composers set up record and publishing companies, and the Performing Right Society allows the composer the chance to collect his own recording and broadcasting fees direct even if he has never been published, there are many targets for the composer's wrath. He will still complain of publishers' antiquated methods, their short-sightedness and failure to promote his works. But since he generally knows there is not much to exploit, he grumbles without much passion. In fact, serious-music publishers often finance serious music with profits from sales of educational, church and popular music.

In the administrative services, middlemen multiply. Today the BBC, the Arts Council, the big opera houses and orchestras all have their secretaries, assistant secretaries, assistant-assistant secretaries, publicity men, consultants on industrial support, personnel managers to keep the complicated musical machine running. Must there be so many? It seems so—for professional music has become institutionalised, has geared itself into the state machine, has made profitable and far-reaching contracts with big business, and in doing so has acquired a sophisticated, highly professionalised, public character.

And what of that most important relationship of all: the relationship of the musician and the public? In Italy and South America, opera singers are still mobbed and fêted, carried shoulder-high through the streets. In central Europe, even orchestral players are highly valued members of society. (In the inter-war years, the Vienna Philharmonic travelled in its own special train with its private wine cellar; during the war, members of the Berlin Philharmonic were preserved as carefully as the nation's art treasures, and were exempted from military service even while the Third Reich was crumbling into ruin.) In Russia, huge crowds gather to welcome pianists returning victorious from yet another international contest. But in England, while poets and novelists, painters and actors, have all in different ages been greatly applauded and honoured, we have no tradition of honouring or supporting musicians. In our own times, we have acquired our musical establishment piecemeal, almost by chance, and without the conscious involvement of the greater part of the population.

And in England, the serious musician still feels a sense of isolation. On the tube, at the sea-front, in the pub or at the airport—wherever he finds himself one of a chance assembly of fellow-beings—he is likely to feel a sense of oppression and separation. How little his work matters to the mass of humanity! How unlikely it is that any of those within earshot have the smallest interest in matters that are of passionate interest to him! No doubt a plumber or an electrician would be as unlikely to find in a chance group other experts with detailed knowledge of sweated joints or alternators. But they would still know that most of the group would be glad, sooner or later, to call on them for service. The musician, as he views the world at large getting on with its business, is always in doubt as to the necessity for his own existence.

Yet over the years, his position has improved out of all knowledge. Music is provided as an amenity and as a matter of course for cultured minorities. Though private patronage has declined, and though English society at large remains generally philistine where music is concerned, the state, representing society, has stepped in and has more than made good the loss. England has discovered the need for a musical heritage—even though the heritage, unlike that of our museums and libraries, in mainly Germanic in origin. We still preserve our ancient puritanical and business instincts; smoking, drinking and gambling are taxed more heavily every year, presumably for the moral as well as the financial good of the nation. It is not so long since music too paid entertainment tax (and not so long since *The Times* listed music under Entertainments rather than under the Arts). Today, it has become a cultural activity, deserving support rather than taxation. And it has also, with the help of radio and recording, become important enough as a potential money-maker to attract well-organised entrepreneurs who bring formidable new skills to the preparation and marketing of the musical product.

*The State steps in*

Important and often disregarded precedents for the subsidisation of music in Britain are to be found in the lower reaches of our musical society. In many cases, activities of the greatest interest to 'serious' music-lovers have sprung from roots in popular or functional music, supported from the start by local councils or by the state, in its role as employer of army bands. There are also precedents for industrial support: from the mid-nineteenth century, many private firms have subsidised their own works bands; though these, like the state-supported cathedral choirs, have for the most part been little involved in mainstream musical activities.

But the municipally supported bands and orchestras of the late nineteenth and early twentieth centuries played a vital part in spreading music—often in an arbitrary and haphazard way—round the country. Many resorts ran what were in fact high-class chamber orchestras.* At Scarborough, Bath, Llandudno or Brighton visitors could hear Mozart and Beethoven symphonies, sometimes played better than they were generally played in the great cities. This was not so surprising, since the best orchestral players in the country spent the summer seasons

* Eric Fenby has recorded that the finest performances of Mozart's late symphonies he ever heard were those given by the Scarborough orchestra under Alick Maclean. Two of England's best orchestral leaders of the '30s and '40s, Paul Beard and David Macallum, had led Maclean's orchestra. Beecham did not disdain to visit Bath (which now supports a piano trio) to conduct the spa orchestra in a programme which included the *Prince Igor* dances.

at the resorts, where they played together regularly in small ensembles under the best of our native conductors; for in the absence of permanent orchestras and opera houses the resorts were the only places where conductors could earn regular salaries and gain necessary experience. In the first decades of this century, the richness and variety of musical life all over England was thus often immeasurably enhanced by state- or council-supported bands and orchestras. Enterprising conductors mounted music festivals—even festivals of British music —with augmented municipal orchestras at New Brighton, Torquay, Scarborough, Eastbourne, Brighton or Hastings.

The army bands supplied professional players to local amateur orchestras, and contributed to their own keep by public appearances. In London, the County Council ran its own bands and, for several years, its own open-air symphony orchestra. The Royal Artillery Orchestra under Ladislav Zavertal performed Wagner's *Meistersinger* Overture in 1868, fourteen years before it appeared on the desks of the Philharmonic Society's orchestra. (Zavertal turned the Artillery orchestra into the finest permanent orchestra in the country; it was he who introduced uniform string bowing to London, long before Lamoureux, who is usually credited with the innovation, arrived there.)

In the 1920s, the resort bandstands, like other seaside castles, proved to have been founded on shifting sand. American dance music drew away younger listeners; car and coach gave holiday-makers a new mobility and put an end to the static holiday. Orchestras were swept away by the rising tide of costs; in times of stress, flower beds and seafront illuminations were judged more attractive as bait to visitors. There was, of course, never a question of state support; no serious-minded, music-loving administrator would have entertained the idea that the tradition of the seaside orchestras was worth preserving.

Yet a precedent had been established, and valuable lessons could have been learnt, if the administrators had been in the mood to learn them. The value of the permanent establishment and of regular rehearsal time was proved. Even where the human material was not of exceptional quality, remarkable results were often obtained through steady and long-maintained effort.

As the gap between popular and serious music grew wider, the chance that a high culture would develop from popular roots became steadily more remote. But in the inter-war years, a new and powerful patron appeared, well-endowed, high-minded, displaying from the first a steady determination to raise the level of taste from above. The British Broadcasting Company, founded in 1922, grew quickly to become the largest employer of musical labour in the country, providing its own salaried musicians with a security and continuity of work they had never known before, and playing a great part in raising standards of performance and educating public taste in what serious musicians recognise as an upward direction. The BBC acted (and still acts) as a patron of independent organisations and musicians; supporting going concerns, making possible concerts of interesting but unpopular music, conducting occasional rescue operations (one of the earliest and most successful was the taking over of the Proms in 1927), commissioning works for broadcasting.

But apart from such direct action, the coming of radio brought about great changes in public attitudes towards music and the ways in which it should be paid for. It was not so much that the BBC gave good value for money, as that the annual licence fee made meaningless established ideas that music should 'pay its way'. The system was quite different from the one which required you to pay out pounds for opera tickets or pennies for deck chairs facing the bandstand. Henceforth, you used music—good, bad or indifferent—as and when you needed it; literally, like water, which is similarly unmetered in England. The listener is no longer paying *his* money for *his* personally selected music; he is paying a subscription for the right to draw on a common stock, and is therefore more tolerant of the idea that the subscription library may contain many sorts of music he himself would never dream of listening to. 'They' provide it, and he is happy (or anyhow acquiescent) in leaving the choice of works and the balancing of the budget to 'them'.

Musicians have been quick to learn the game of precedents. Once the principle of *music as public service* is established, the game of leapfrog begins. What has been done once can be done again. If music can be provided as a municipal service or by a broadcasting company, why not also as a state service? If army bands can be used to sustain the morale of civilians, why cannot civilian entertainers be used to sustain the troops? If ENSA can provide wartime entertainment for the army, why should not CEMA provide a slightly more cultural sort of entertainment for the rest of us? And so, from the Council for the Encouragement of Music and the Arts, which started life supported only by a grant from the charitable Pilgrim Trust, the Arts Council was born.

Parallels can be drawn with other subsidised arts and services by musicians within the administrative services. 'If we admit as we do a social necessity to spend £16,000,000 a year on our public libraries, how can we allow our comparable expenditure on music, drama, opera and ballet to shrink to about one-twelfth of that figure?' 'If the taxpayer subsidises eggs at ten shillings a year, should he grudge tenpence a year spent on the Arts?' (Arts Council reports). There is the appeal to patriotism: 'How is it that the Berlin Philharmonic receives a subsidy four times as large as that of any English orchestra, the Swedish town of Gavle gives its orchestra a subsidy nearly twice as big as the LSO's guarantees from Arts Council and Greater London Council combined?'

Newcomers lever themselves into the system by quoting precedents. If the National Youth Orchestra deserves a grant, why not the National Youth Brass Band? If contemporary chamber music is sponsored by the Arts Council's Contemporary Music Network, why not jazz? And why not early music? Sometimes ambition overleaps itself; but many points are successfully made. It is the successes which count; for there is a sort of ratchet action involved in subsidy. A public body rarely reverses its policy in matters of subsidy; to do so is to admit one's errors and to lose face.

What are the motives that lead private patrons, industry or the state to support music? Private patrons are often motivated equally by love of music and love of *réclame*—it can never be disagreeable to be at the centre of an artistic milieu, praised and thanked by artists and public. The industrial patrons who succeed them are mainly concerned with the *réclame*—it is a popular delusion that most industrial patronage schemes are really tax-evasion schemes in disguise. They will admit freely that a sponsored festival may generate more good will and attract more public attention than a full-page advertisement in the national press, which could be bought for about the same price. But often (as in the old municipal councils at Bournemouth and elsewhere) the presence of one or two force-ful music-lovers in positions of influence seems to sway the balance towards music and away from recreation grounds for young people or afforestation schemes, when industries are deciding how to demonstrate their general benevolence and concern for society. The reasons why governments allocate money to the arts are more complex; but even here I doubt very much that many decisions are coolly made on a rational political level.

Musicians, playing the leapfrog game, regularly complain of their niggardly treatment by the government of the day; yet on a rational basis, it is hard to see why government should support the arts at all. After many years of musical education in state and private schools, there is no evidence that music has a positive effect on character. Serious music is not a particularly valuable export, considered in terms of foreign exchange. Governments may support serious music partly for the same reasons as they support army bands: to boost morale; to help the tourist trade; and to show foreigners that all is still well with the old country. But I believe that our arts administrators are for the most part genuine and passionate believers in the abstract value of 'good' music. Not since the time of Albert the Prince Consort have musicians been able to count on so much sympathy, support and understanding in high places. Many of our administrators, who in the nineteenth century might have been ardent spare-time archaeologists, classical scholars, or patrons of painting and sculpture, are today equally ardent music-lovers; their conviction of music's central value to humanity all the greater in an age when other faiths have lost their hold. For music—soul-enlarging, apt for ritual and ceremonial, politically non-controversial—today supplies for many the place which religion once held. And most of those who are not particularly musical—like lapsed church-goers who would still be deeply shocked by any attempt to demote the Archbishop of Canterbury or secularise the Church—are glad that the best musical products should be made available, as long as they are not asked to sample them themselves.

Of course, no one is ever satisfied with the way the system works. Smaller regional companies complain of the huge share of the income available that goes to prestigious national companies; chamber orchestras and contemporary music groups complain at the amount given to symphony orchestras which churn out the same classics week after week. Composers demand a protective quota system and point out how much more other countries do for their own composers. The members of experimental groups not yet under the state umbrella cry out against the mandarins who take the important decisions knowing nothing of the new, vital movements that could, with a little encouragement, transform the face of music, and produce their own recipes for the artistic salvation of the state.*

Arts councils, like state broadcasting corporations and charitable subsidising organisations, suffer from certain defects which are common to all large, centrally controlled organisations responsible for doling out public money. They tend to be cautious, slow to move, somewhat insulated from movements at the periphery, dedicated to their own smoothly running systems as well as to music and musicians. They tend to reflect the spirit and beliefs of the musical establishment (identifiable in the pronouncements of university professors, heads of conservatoires, senior critics of the quality press) and are a little too conscious of their roles as upholder of 'standards' and leaders of public taste. (Stephen Plaistow, formerly head of BBC music programmes, probably thought that he was expressing a self-evident truth when he wrote: 'Public taste must, of course, be led.')

The British Arts Council, unlike many subsidising organisations on both sides of the Iron Curtain, is neither corrupt nor given to nepotism. Serious musicians recognise it as their ally in the battle against indifference and philistinism, even when they grumble at the ways in which it sets to work. Like other large, public commissioning bodies it prides itself on its fair-mindedness. Yet it is very doubtful if fair-mindedness always operates to the good of the musical state. Patrons who follow their hunches, publishers who promote a few hopeful composers at the expense of others equally hopeful, are not fair-minded but often achieve more for new music than the official bodies which feel morally bound to provide equal chances for all who

* The most bizarre recipe was given by David Castillejo in his *Counter Report on Art Patronage* (1968): 'If Covent Garden was closed down for one year *only* . . . and the money redirected to the creation of new art, I calculate that this one year could produce, in a random list, about fifty new symphonies, commissioned and performed (one a week); *plus* a hundred new plays commissioned and performed (two a week); *plus* the year's work of fifty painters; *plus* about three or four full-scale operas commissioned and performed; *plus* ten large-scale poetry anthologies; *plus* fifty novels commissioned and published (one a week).'

are equally worthy.* Dole out two biscuit crumbs a day to every member of the shipwrecked crew, and the whole lot may die of starvation—yet what other course can a fair-minded captain follow?

Old-style patrons often knew all too well what they liked and disliked, and the composers or performers they employed chafed under the conditions and restrictions imposed on them. But at least contact was maintained between supplier and consumer. In an age of subsidy, the commissioning of music and the choice of programmes is often left in the hands of enlightened middlemen—the more 'musical' they are, the less likely they are to be on the wavelength of the hypothetical listener; already distanced by radio and recording. Arts Councils are aware of this difficulty, and tend to subsidise performing groups which already have access to established audiences. But the predicament of composers is more serious. When a composer knows that his work will be selected by panels, committees of new-music societies, competition juries—all composed of knowledgeable musicians—he tends to write for his peers rather than for the general public. The hypothetical listener recedes still further into the background, the composer aims high and hopes for the best. And often when his work comes to performance, the lay listener, standing hopefully in the line of fire, hears the whine of bullets passing overhead, and cannot display even a hole in his hatbrim when the battle is over.

A further defect of the system may appear as no defect at all to the high-minded. The subsidisation of high art inevitably involves the penalisation of middle-brow art and the further-narrowing and segregating of cultural activities. Operetta, concerts of popular classics, entertainment music of all sorts, are left to the commercial managements, which are forced to skimp on rehearsal time and production costs in an effort to keep out of the red. 'Commercial' concerts move off down-market in search of larger audiences, and serious music becomes still more serious—we are deprived of vital ingredients

* William Glock, when he was controller of BBC music, was consistently accused of favouring the composers of the second Viennese school at the expense of others; Lina Lalandi made no attempt to 'balance' the programmes of the English Bach Festivals, and forced us to listen to Messiaen and Xenakis at a time when most of us neither knew nor cared about them; Boosey and Hawkes promoted Britten's music as single-mindedly as Unilever would promote a new washing powder.

in our diet which should be essential to a healthy and balanced musical life.

Those who have made it to the top without state support often question the need for any subsidy at all. Ives would have given the young composer a field to dig rather than a scholarship; Stravinsky called for a Ford Foundation for the suppression of Unpromising Composers. Perhaps the greatest composers will always emerge from the hardest backgrounds, as the greatest prizefighters have emerged from the ranks of the underprivileged and deprived slum-dwellers of London and New York—if so, we had better make our minds up to do without great composers, as we have made our minds up to do without castrati.

There is the risk that performers who are also state employees will become too comfortable in their jobs. Players in operahouse and broadcasting orchestras or in army bands may stay in the same cosy niche for their whole working lives. Their appetite for adventure may atrophy, they may fall victim to routine. But in a mixed economy, most musical organisations rely on many income sources for their living. Army bands supplement their pay by appearing on public bandstands and at garden parties; opera companies and orchestras depend not only on state subsidies, but on industrial patronage; on impresarios, film or record companies who hire them; and of course on the public which buys tickets at the box office. If their members are to live comfortably, they need to maintain income from all sources at a healthy level. So in fact, very few musicians in subsidised bodies have the same sort of security as most civil servants enjoy. They are in the precarious position of the owners of sophisticated central-heating systems; it only needs a failure or threat of strike action in water, gas or electricity industries for the whole system to be put out of action. In addition, the musician who relies on subsidy becomes the hostage of all sorts of political and economic forces of which he has little knowledge and over which he has no control. He benefits at the moment; but there are too many precedents for the collapse of apparently stout parties for him ever to look forward confidently to a secure future.

Subsidy having become part of our national way of life, it is difficult to remember how things went in the bad old days of free-for-all, expensive-for-some, profit-and-loss making music.

Music has passed into the class of 'essential luxuries' identified by the economist David White: in hard times, we need such luxuries more than ever as symbols of hope and survival, and of the good life that we hope will soon return. Music, like chocolate, is instantly enjoyable; depression is *now*, and music offers immediate release into an ideal world where problems are posed only to be resolved. A good concert is a symbol of good living—not expensive in absolute terms, but without question 'the best of its sort'. A ticket for the opera, far from carrying a government health warning as cigarettes do, bears an implicit recommendation in the form of a subsidy. We can even feel virtuous while we are enjoying the luxury, as we might if we supported British industry by buying a new car from Leyland.

We can be grateful that government acknowledges a responsibility to provide serious music as a service to the community; but we need not be too grateful. It is because the amount of subsidy involved is small that government can afford to be generous. In the areas of housing, food or old age pensions, the subsidies involved are so large that generosity can only be achieved by painful sacrifices in other sectors. But the needs of the small yet vocal public for the arts can be met, satisfied, and even encouraged to grow, without any major disturbance of economic balance. The quality press make sure that all developments in this field are well advertised; politicians are pleased to be seen patting the head of a mild cultural beast, with a healthily small appetite.

For though audiences for serious music have increased, they are still a tiny minority. The fact that radio listeners pay nothing for their music programmes has less to do with the value of music than with the insignificant size of listening groups; it is not worth while collecting a separate licence fee from them. The fact that the public will only buy concert tickets if half the cost is supplied by government or industry, while they will buy whisky taxed up to five or six times its untaxed value, is a sign that the demand for whisky is a good deal more imperious than the demand for music. If the rate of absenteeism went up when Haitink plays Mahler as it goes up when Arsenal play Queens Park Rangers, music-lovers might well find that their pleasures were taxed instead of being subsidised.

Yet the dedicated few, for whom music is a passion, an addiction, a way of life, should not be too despondent. Today, they have powerful allies on their side. Radio and recording advertise their cause; reinforce the message by endless repetitions; spread it around the world. A grand alliance has been formed between music and commerce, making it possible for music to enter our lives and intertwine with our everyday thoughts and actions as it has never done before. The surface changes in the musician's way of life may have been surprisingly small, but in the last fifty years the world has changed about him. Electronic technology, like a boulder thrown into a stream which has for centuries followed the same course, is creating a new environment: new currents, new whirlpools, and new still backwaters. The stream breaks its banks to irrigate new lands, while places that were once fertile are now left dry and arid.

## III

### MUSIC AND TECHNOLOGY

To discern the most fruitful uses of an invention is to take a great imaginative step into the future. The entrepreneurs who recognised the biro's potential as a throw-away fountain pen and who adapted plastic bags for use as disposable binliners had a touch of genius in their make-up: they supplied needs of which the public had not even been aware before they came along. But many inventions have a complicated early history of misapplication and frustrated development. Inventors are like fond parents who send their children to one school after another in the hope that their potential may be recognised and encouraged to bloom—all too often, they turn out to have no potential at all.

Of course, there are inventions that leap, Athene-like, from the brains of their creators, fully formed and ready for specific uses. The zip-fastener and the cat's-eye reflector belong to this class. There are even a few musical inventions which were produced to meet particular problems to which they instantly provided the right answers. Certain valve and key mechanisms for woodwind and brass, cello spikes, and folding music stands come into this group. Against these successes, we must enter up all the magnetic page-turners, patent finger-exercisers, transparent musical blackboards which are launched into the world with fanfares, then fade into oblivion in the small-ad columns of the musical press.

Like the tailor in the fairy story who wins the race by jumping on to the giant's back, the musician often takes advantage of technical developments in alien fields—in fact, he rarely has the special skills or the money needed to do much in the technological field himself. Iron-framed pianos, high-tension steel strings and nylon strings were the by-products of high-powered industrial research. The prototype of one of the later reproducing pianos was made largely from parts used in the Link simulated-flight aviation trainer; the smallest violin in the new 'family of strings' designed for the Catgut Acoustical Society of America is strung with parachute nylon.

And the most revolutionary of all musical aids, the phonograph and radio, were first developed and exploited for use in non-musical fields. Radio was thought of as offering a cheaper alternative to land-lines in underdeveloped countries; the phonograph was marketed as an office dictaphone, and then as an amusement-arcade entertainer. The microphone and thermionic valve were developed in telephone research; the computers used in electronic music are descendants of computers designed for information storage and calculation. In all these cases, it took time, imagination, and many failed attempts, before the possible implications of these technological developments for music were at all understood.

*Medium in search of a character*
The speed with which the gramophone won acceptance in serious-music circles and laid the foundations of a respectable repertoire was due to the fact that many forces were working in the same direction. The line of advance—towards ever more faithful reproduction—was clearly mapped out; and change was not inhibited by rigidity at high levels, as it was in long-established opera houses, concert-giving societies, conservatoires and university music departments. The gramophone industry adopted the same sort of forceful promotion methods which had formerly been used to sell pianos and mechanical pianos. But the piano manufacturers had been working within a known context and improving on a known situation, in which an already expanding market was waiting to be tapped; while the recording industry inherited no traditions. It created its own public, and evolved its own codes of conduct or misconduct in the process.* Very quickly, a casual relationship between technology and music developed into a close-knit and finally indissoluble alliance, in which neither music nor Mammon ruled unchallenged. The musician, with his invisible capital of traditional skills and stiffened by an artistic conscience, still wielded decisive influence; but neither party could advance

* Its early employers were not so much unmusical as (in a business sense) a-musical. Record scouts such as Fred Gaisberg not only scoured Italy, Hungary and Russia for new talent; they visited India, China and Japan, ready to record any sounds that might be of commercial value. In the process, and almost incidentally, they opened up the frontiers between the nations of the world, extending the narrow boundaries of Western culture quite as effectively as the ethno-musicologists of later decades.

without consultation and cooperation with the other. High-minded and low-minded (or business-minded) men combined to set in motion processes of evolution new to the world of music. Two impinging forces had produced a resultant force stronger and more effective than either would have been on its own.

'Recording', said Schnabel, 'is the destruction of music.' Musicians' initial suspicions of the new medium sprang from several different roots. There was an element of instinctive fear that the recording machine, like the camera, can steal away a part of the victim's identity. There was an element of reaction against the brash claims of the technologists: as late as 1913, Edison declared that 'Music is in the same backward state that electricity was forty years ago. I am going to develop it. I hope to complete the task in three years.' There were more practical fears that recording would misrepresent their art, and that, if the market was flooded with cheap imitations, there would be no demand for the real thing.

Yet from the early 1900s there were always first-rank musicians willing to record. The human voice recorded better than most instruments, which was lucky, as most opera singers were not purists in matters of authentic accompaniment or the use of uncut versions, and were easily won over by the prospect of large rewards* and free advertisement. Famous stars had no reason to fear comparisons with the machine that was, at first, hardly more than a toy. The 'real' music was still the music of live performance. The faults of the singer could even be blamed on the apparatus; when the ageing Patti recorded in her retirement, admirers blamed the machine for all the imperfections.

Recalling the gramophone's origins in the world of light entertainment, it is not so surprising to find that many of the conductors, composers and instrumentalists who recorded before the 1920s had connections in this world. Landon Ronald, one of the first conductors of repute to work in the recording industry, was the son of a ballad-singer and himself a composer of popular ballads. Nikisch, who conducted the Berlin Philharmonic Orchestra on a record of Beethoven's Fifth Symphony in 1914, recalled that his earliest musical experiences had been of Rossini overtures played on an orchestrion, or mechanical orchestra. Elgar, who became enthusiastic about recording

* By 1921, Caruso had earned more than £400,000 from his recordings.

during the First World War, had grown up in a provincial world where light overtures, selections and pot-pourris formed a major part of the musical diet.

In our less permissive age, we have to make an effort to understand how great conductors could have connived at the cutting down of masterworks and their re-scoring with metal-horned Stroh violins backing up the Strads, clarinets supporting violas, and tubas replacing double-basses. Elgar conducted four-minute versions of his *Cockaigne* overture and of the slow movement of his Violin Concerto; Weingartner hustled through the slow movement of Beethoven's Fifth Symphony knocking minutes off his usual timing so as to get it on to two sides of a twelve-inch record. But the moral climate even of the 1920s was very different from today's; and in fact it is largely because of radio and recording that the atmosphere has changed, so that we now expect to hear works complete, and in their original orchestration. Today, we take Puccini and Kreisler to task for having composed arias or violin *morceaux* to the four-and-a-half-minute module. It is easy enough for us to be moral now that such shifts and compromises are no longer necessary. But who knows how things would have gone if technological advance had stopped in the 1920s? We might by now have a large repertory of four-and-a-half-minute masterworks for brass bands, choir boys, and tubular bells, and the theorists would be busily explaining that these developments were implicit in the music of Beethoven, Brahms and Wagner.

The evolution of the gramophone was hastened in the 1920s and '30s by the need to keep pace with radio, which early in its history offered better sound reproduction and freedom from time limitations; and by the depression which hit player-piano and record industries with equal force. American record sales fell from 104,000,000 in 1927 to 6,000,000 in 1932, phonograph sales from 987,000 to 40,000 in the same period. The pianola, with its bona fide piano mechanism, had in its earlier career won much more respect from most musicians than the phonograph; in the 1920s, the London colleges of music were still installing player-pianos, and as late as 1925 the BBC were considering the discontinuance of all record programmes and the substitution of player-piano music. But the end of the boom came with horrid suddenness. American pianola sales fell from a peak of 205,556 in 1923 to 2,171 in 1931, then to 418 in 1935; after which time, many mechanical pianos ended their lives on giant bonfires. For the player-piano, 'perfected' as the reproducing piano, was too perfect, and also too delicate, to survive. Finding no riposte or possibility of self-improvement or of escaping from its own character, it became extinct.

The gramophone, however, was still only at the Neanderthal stage of evolution. With the introduction of electrical recording in the mid-1920s, it gained the power to compete on equal terms with radio in matters of fidelity. Automatic record-changing and, later, the LP allowed records to offer uninterrupted and effort-free listening. The equipment needed was not exactly simple, but was both simple and robust compared with the amazingly complicated and delicate pneumatic mechanisms of the more sophisticated reproducing pianos.

A few years after the introduction of electrical recording, almost every sound in the conventional musical vocabulary could be reproduced faithfully enough to give pleasure to most discriminating music-lovers. Thinking back, I do not believe that many of us in the 1930s envisaged anything much better than some of Beecham's or Walter's earlier recordings. But a competitive industry must advance if it is to stay in the same place. And so, inevitably, electrical recording blossomed into full-frequency and hi-fi; stereo and quadraphonic sound followed, each development leading to massive re-recording programmes and equally massive sales of new equipment. The musical gains were real, though less important to ordinary listeners than they were made out to be by their promoters. The faithful servant was performing his duties more zealously and exactly than ever; but a suspicion was creeping in that musicians were being conned—taken for a ride in a direction they would never haven chosen for themselves.

Today, the record companies are one of the major powers in the musical state. The solvency of many major orchestras depends on their record contracts, and the choice of a new conductor will be closely linked with the recording contracts he can bring with him. Record companies will reject key players in orchestras and often bring about their replacement. They will form their own recording orchestras, as Walter Legge of EMI formed the Philharmonia in 1945, and will try to disband them as Walter Legge did in 1964 (but, as Proust said, 'it is easier to create a great work of art than to destroy it', and the Philharmonia survived). Recording programmes come to be as important as concert programmes, and will often dictate their content. Soloists' reputations are made by their records almost as often as by their live appearances. The draw of the recording star is almost as great in opera house or concert hall as the draw of the TV star who appears at the Palladium or at the local repertory theatre. In the pop world, the record is often the 'real thing', the live performance the replica. Though we are nowhere near that position yet in the serious-music world, we are much nearer to it than we were twenty years ago. Pessimists may look forward to the time when live performers will be like brewers' dray-horses—admired survivors of a past age; kept for advertisement rather than for practical use, and exhibited by grace and favour of the proprietors on May Days and public holidays.

In fact, I don't believe we shall ever reach that point. For we have already gone beyond the stage where we can sensibly talk of the live concert as the 'real thing' and the record as the replica, or imagine that position reversed, so that the record is the 'real thing'. The recorded performance is beginning to develop a life of its own; we listen to it and assess it in its own right. And the live performance has changed character in response to the influence of its recorded counterpart. Yet the image of master-and-servant remains, sanctified by all the jargon of hi-fi, of faithful reproduction, of the 'aura' and 'presence' of the concert hall supposedly reproduced on the record.

*Imperfect, pluperfect: two faces of music*
There seem to be three main reasons why 'fidelity' should be a problem word. First: because of its history of exaggerated and indiscriminate use in advertising; commerce comes in at the door and truth flies out of the window. Second: because judgement of what constitutes adequate recording changes continually as recording techniques evolve. Third: because musicians are committed to a view of the recording industry as 'music's faithful servant' and are psychologically incapable of recognising that recorded music may develop its own independent role. Don Quixote, blinded by his vision of the ideal Dulcinea, was unable to see the real girl; and musicians are unable to see the electronic media except in the roles they have assigned to them.

According to publicity handouts, there never was such a

thing as lo-fi. The phonograph of 1902 'imitated any and every musical instrument faithfully'. By 1908: 'step by step the gramophone has been perfected ... every possible defect has been eliminated.' If you doubt the sincerity of the Edison-Bell Company or of *Cassell's Magazine*, you have Patti's word for it that (in 1906) 'though the old records they took of my voice were very good, those which they are now bringing out are just perfect'. In 1914, Nikisch reported on his Fifth Symphony recording that 'the reproduction of instrumental music was absolutely true from an artistic standpoint'.

Advertisers have their own standards of truthfulness; and no soloists recording a disc or cutting a pianola roll can afford to be less than ecstatic in public testimonials. Yet Conan Doyle allowed the astute Moriarty to be taken in by a recording of Holmes's violin, and his readers never raised a protest. Presumably early record buyers accepted the sounds on their merits because they had no valid standards of comparison. The immediate sounds drove out vague and imperfect memories of past experiences. But surely experienced music-lovers could not be so easily satisfied?

One answer seems to be that even the scratchiest and most distorted recordings of small-frequency range give many clues to articulation, tempo fluctuations, balance and so on, which were of incredible interest to the listener and monopolised his full attention. The 'truth' Nikisch perceived may not have been the whole truth, but was still of unique value. Full-frequency recording, stereo and quadraphonic sound would widen the range of information made available, but this did not lessen the value of information supplied by early records. The value of the distorted recording is probably even greater to the experienced listener; like the expert on ancient manuscripts, he becomes skilled in reading through the mysterious signs, illegible to others, to get at the sense behind.

Yet once we have become used to 'better' recordings, we can hardly understand how we ever could have borne the earlier ones. It is the recordings themselves that have created our standards; if old techniques had not been superseded, we might still accept the standards of the past without complaint.

The record industry developed necessary techniques during the first 35 years of the century as rapidly and purposefully as a strongly-motivated pupil learning an instrument. The targets are clearly set; early advances from zero point to a reasonable state of competence are gratifyingly obvious. But whereas the pianist's curve of achievement soon flattens out, and it becomes clear that he will never get past the asymptote fixed by his own limitations, there seems to be no end to the 'improvement' of recording processes. Long ago they broke through the ceiling of perfection, and soared on upwards into regions of 'better than perfect'. That is to say, the record today offers us something 'better' than we are likely to hear in the concert hall or opera house. Instruments can be brought into the foreground by use of spot-microphones so that we can hear detail as we never hear it in the concert hall. If the acoustics of a concert hall are not right for the music, they can be modified or suppressed by selective filtering processes. Middle frequencies can be stepped up to increase what the engineers call 'presence'. String tone can be given a smoothness and sheen unlike anything to be heard in the concert hall. Already in the 1930s, Stokowski was recording on eight channels; the completed work could then be assembled in whatever ways the conductor chose, so that 'performance' became a matter of as much care and deliberation as composition. Karajan recorded Schoenberg's *Orchestral Variations* with the orchestra re-seated for every variation to improve the balance and clarity of sound. The use of magnetic tape has made possible many other special effects produced by overlapping or combining separate tracks. At every point, electronic treatment of natural sounds is possible, ranging from hardly noticeable manipulations of timbre or dynamic to the crudest echo-chamber effects.

At what point do we decide that the faithful servant is exceeding his duties? In serious-music circles, we are reluctant to admit that any change wrought by electronic means on live sound can be a change for the better. Colin Mawby speaks for the purists: 'It is so easy to solve difficulties of balance through the skilful use of microphone technique that records sometimes give a completely false picture of what a piece actually sounds like ... recorded sound is never going to be as good as the real thing.' Stravinsky, in his eighties, declared: 'Natural balance, natural dynamics, natural echo, natural colour, natural human error: these have been replaced by added echo and reverberation, by a neutralizing dynamic range, by filtered sound, by an engineered balance.... The resulting record is a super-glossy, chem-fab music-substitute never heard on sea or land, or even in Philadelphia.' Even those who work in the classical-music departments of record companies claim that they accept the standards of the concert hall as their norm, and admit to no higher ambition than to capture the spirit of the live concert in their recordings.

Cynics will point out that it is in their interest on commercial as well as on moral-aesthetic grounds to take this line. The geese that lay so many golden eggs for the record companies must be treated with care and respect. And so, when the technicians do improve on live performances, they do it with discretion. On major issues, they play fair. We rightly believe that if we are promised Menuhin playing unaccompanied Bach we won't hear the lower notes of triple-stopped passages discreetly touched in by a second anonymous player. But the aulty top Cs of famous opera singers have sometimes been supplied by other voices, and wrong notes are corrected as they once were on the reproducing-piano rolls. The technicians are as ingenious and circumspect as gardeners who exhibit at county shows, injecting wax under the skins of their giant marrows or polishing the cucumbers with secret mixtures to enhance their glossiness—but never beyond the point at which the judges will suspect the tricks and subterfuges that have gone to produce such unnaturally perfect bloom and ripeness.

And sounds, like exhibition fruit, can be too perfect, too glossily finished off, for everyday use. We may also question the reproduction through stereo of some of the least significant acoustic circumstances of musical experience when the whole repertory is indiscriminately recorded in stereo and then again in quadraphony. I rather resent the superfidelity forced on us in the form of expensive new equipment and the recordings that go with it, as I resent the fitted carpets and electric cigar lighter I am forced to buy with my mass-produced car. But the record industry must be seen to advance, and is committed to one single line of advance. Recorded music must be a little more than lifelike and twice as natural. The industry and the (serious) musicians it employs generally concur in treating the live sounds as sacred, and shy away from the idea that the medium itself might play a significant part in shaping the end-product.

Serious musicians, steeped in tradition and sacred memories, may tolerate Moog-synthesised Bach once in a while, as a joke against themselves. But they are apt to be deeply suspicious of modifications of natural sounds in non-joke contexts. They have grown up with a great respect for the 'natural' characters of instruments, and regard the sound of souped-up violins or electronically amplified basses as an affront to their natures. Performers and habitual concert-goers are connoisseurs of live sounds, and are as incapable of appreciating artificial tastes in music as the epicure who knows the taste of fresh peaches is of appreciating tinned peaches (which may well be even preferable to the innocent palate). At a practical level, the performer is also suspicious of electronic aids which, in their present state of development, often prove to be crude and unreliable. So he too sets his face against any change in the *status quo*.

Yet, surreptitiously, recording is evolving its own standards which are not identical with those of the concert hall, and attracting listeners who approach music in a new way. The hi-fi listener who loves to wrap himself round with sound is enjoying a distinct and separate sort of musical experience. Concert-goers sometimes feel excluded from the pleasures and preoccupations of hi-fi listeners; but it does not follow that they are themselves superior, or that the record listener is taking a route to musical enjoyment that is somehow illicit.

We seem to be witnessing the beginnings of the same sort of evolution that has already taken place in the world of pop music. Here, it is accepted that the record exists in its own right, and may be better than the real thing—if the 'real thing' exists at all. Recording techniques are used to modify and enlarge on live performances in ways that are not merely cosmetic, but truly creative. The record often sets the standard, and the concert performer, bereft of studio aids and technical advisers, tries his best to live up to the reputation of the idealized self already known to the audience from disc or tape.

Already there are plenty of singers and players who do in fact sound better on record than they ever do in the concert hall; nor do I see (in theory) why we should think less of a recording artist who fails to make good in live performance than we do of a concert performer who is acoustically and temperamentally out of his element in the recording studio. If the engineers can manufacture better singers, or better orchestras, for us by the exercise of their arts, we should accept gratefully what they have to offer. If they let us hear inner parts in Beethoven or Mahler symphonies we have never heard before, we should accept that too. And if they even go beyond that point, and devise new ways of presenting old works which display them in strange lights, we should at least preserve open minds till we have heard them out. There is no reason why recorded music should remain for ever the mirror-image of live music. It is developing its own character, surreptitiously but distinctly. And on the face of concert music, we can already detect a new expression, which signifies its own reaction to the changed image of itself presented by the reproducing media.

Sensory, emotional, and aesthetic pleasures are rarely if ever encountered in a pure and unmixed state. Experience is many-levelled, and may well contain contradictory and antagonistic elements (we can enjoy our breakfast while we mourn the death of a favourite aunt). 'Pure' musicians maintain that they go to concerts for the music alone,* but for most of us there is no such thing as 'pure' musical experience. Just as we respond to the atmosphere of a restaurant: a mysterious concoction of décor, lighting, seating arrangements, the friendliness or remoteness of waiters and fellow-customers, so in the concert hall we are influenced by certain $x$-factors: catalysts or inhibiting agents which colour and affect our experience of the music itself.

The most obvious $x$-factor in a live performance is the visual accompaniment to the musical experience: which supplements hearing, providing pointers which aid understanding, or offers alternative entertainment as we view hyperactive conductors or perspiring bass players. A further factor is the sense of involvement which follows when many people, at some expense of energy and cash, have got themselves to the right place at the right time in order to share an experience which is at once celebration, ritual, and affirmation of togetherness. Then again, there is the sense of commitment to a quasi-monastic retreat. We have separated ourselves from the world, shut ourselves deliberately in a soundproof shrine where telephones never ring and children never cry for attention. There is the sense of immediacy: we are where the action is, standing on the knife-edge between past and future, relishing the delights of uncertainty and weighing possible delight against possible disappointment. The last and most mysterious $x$-factor is the aura of reality. The 'real thing' has a mystical value for us because it

* Ernest Newman even maintained that the greatest and *purest* pleasure of all was to stay at home and read the score. Yet he remained an avid concert-goer till the end of his days.

is the real thing. We will queue to hear Menuhin or Rostropovich as we once queued to see the moon-dust, or as pilgrims travel for many months to touch the sacred relics. Even if the great man is off form, and we cannot hear much from our seats at the back of the cathedral, the time was not wasted. We have been in the presence of greatness, and will never come closer to the true, inimitable reality.

The $x$-factors for live music are quite distinct from the $y$-factors which enhance our enjoyment of recorded music. These include: technical perfection that surpasses real-life perfection; greater clarity of detail; the guarantee against disappointment (the record cannot let you down, the live performer who suffers from migraine, sore throat, and unsympathetic colleagues can, and does). The record-fan has his own musical games. He may play the comparison game: weighing one performance against another, acquiring an expertise in judging fine points of interpretation which concert-goers, for ever listening to unique, evanescent performances, cannot hope to rival. The technically-minded come to terms with music almost by the way, in caring for their sound-systems. Hi-fi enthusiasts are often as sensitive to the state of their equipment's health as the owners of vintage cars are to the smooth running of their engines, and may prefer to run on two-star Rachmaninov rather than on four-star Beethoven if that is the way to get the best out of the system.

Concert-goers are not in a strong position to condemn record-users for playing the comparisons game or for being more interested in their equipment than in the music. The record-user finds his way into the musical experience by means of his games just as the concert-goer does through his interest in the visual and psychological musical additives of live performance. No one can stomach distilled water, free of all those impurities which give it taste and flavour.

The live performer can never rival the technical perfection of the record, the record can never capture the freshness and immediacy of live performance. But record companies are aware of the significance of the missing $x$-factors, and make some effort to compensate for their loss. The position here is not straightforward, for recording engineers have for long been committed to the flawless, hygienically perfect performance: a *specialité de la maison* not to be lightly abandoned. Conductors and engineers have their professional pride which drives them on to achieve technical perfection and to eliminate every blemish and wart on the fair countenance of the music they present, justifying their action by maintaining that flaws which are tolerable in live performance become intolerable on repetition. In fact, it is doubtful if the public care half as much about technical perfection as recording men or record reviewers. We treasure our imperfect old 78s and are no more worried by the occasional smudged passage or split horn note than we are by the false starts, split notes, shouts of players high on drugs or alcohol which we accept as part of the necessary acoustic dirt on recordings of New Orleans jazz.

Today, many recording engineers have abandoned the sort of tape-surgery common a few years ago, which never left a good performance alone. It would be interesting to test the results if they went a stage further, and if the producer, after due setting-up and rehearsal, were to say to the performers: 'Stand by—we record the Choral Symphony *now*, for better or worse, and that is the version that will go out to the public. If the oboe messes his solo or the balance man misses a cue, that's too bad.' But professional self-respect could never allow such a thing to happen.

*Influences and cross-influences*
The most obvious changes to have come about through the influence of radio and recording have been in standards and style of performance. Good news of great performers spreads instantly through the sounds themselves. New standards are set, and new ideas and fashions quickly propagated. Performance styles become increasingly internationalised and homogenised; Russian, German, American, English, and even French orchestras have lost many of their national characteristics over the last thirty or forty years. At the same time, even students can become experienced in all sorts of music as they never could in the past; they learn from records and radio more or less how a Machaut motet or Schoenberg's *Pierrot Lunaire* should sound, and in no time at all are themselves giving meaningful and idiomatic performances. If the National Youth Orchestra can sound like a world-famous orchestra when they play *Rite of Spring* under Boulez, it is partly because they have grown up with the sounds of world-famous orchestras in their ears.

The electronic media have changed the professional's approach to public music-making. No longer can he treat each concert as a matter for himself and the audience of the day alone. He must think of the unseen, anonymous audience, and of the possibility that his performance may be examined and analysed in detail and at leisure by unknown critics and (most alarming of all) by fellow-performers. He can no more afford to take risks than the politicians who are followed round the country by reporters armed with notebooks and tape-recorders.

For practical reasons, the recording or radio artist must aim at consistency and accuracy before almost all else. Editing processes have brought great flexibility to recording, and it is no longer necessary to record in four-and-a-half-minute stretches once-for-always; but the high costs of recording mean that preference is always likely to be given to the reliable man who gets it right first time. Record companies cannot afford to re-record an orchestral passage four or five times for the sake of a temperamental player who may give the performance of his life the fifth time.

Radio and recording do not so much create their own performers, as filter off those who are temperamentally at their best in the studio, and whose style and timbre suit the medium. In the early days of recording, relatively few came through the test with success. Even today, there are many fine performers whose art does not translate into the new media. But because connections between radio, recording, and live concert-giving are so close, and because fame in one field helps to build up a reputation in the two others, solo performers who are rejected by radio or recording are rarely able to make their names in the concert hall either.

The electronic media also filter off and select their own repertory of music. In the old days, whistlers, brass bands and singers dominated the record catalogues, because they could be recorded with reasonably good results. In the same way, when stereo came in, there was a vogue for music-in-space. Bands marched across the living room, and Beethoven's 'Battle' Symphony was revived so that we could enjoy the cannon to right of them, cannon to left of them. Once on record, the symphony even made its way on occasion into the concert hall; the records having created a demand for live performances. Kurt Blaukopf attributes the Mahler revival to stereo, which has allowed us to sort out the complex textures and to appreciate chamber-music nuances in an orchestral context more easily than in the concert hall—though in Mahler's case many other factors are also involved.

The recording of vast works like the Mahler *Song of the Earth*, with the innumerable rehearsal periods that are necessary, is possible because profits continue to flow in over many years from all over the world. It also becomes economically worthwhile to record esoteric and specialist music, which can be distributed to a thinly spread world audience and in time recoup the original outlay. As Jacques Barzun has said: 'The whole literature of one of the arts has come into being—it is like the Renaissance rediscovering the ancient classics and holding them fast by means of the printing press.'

Recording has turned out to be an apt medium both for the most demanding and for the least demanding music. Difficult modern works come into their own when listeners can repeat the performance *ad infinitum*. Even from an economic point of view, you could say that the Viennese atonalists offer good value for money. You buy their music, dense with meaning and guaranteed free from repeated passages, and supply reinforcing repetitions at no extra cost. At the other end of the spectrum, there is an ever-growing recorded repertory of music by minor masters of the eighteenth and nineteenth centuries which we would not make the effort to hear in the concert hall but which pleasantly whiles away the passing hour, or provides material for half-listening at home. The gramophone has taken over and expanded the repertory of overtures, suites, light-classical tone poems and symphonies which used to enliven our concert programmes; a glance at the prospectus for any concert season before the 1950s will reveal how the picture has changed.

As the cinema industry, threatened by TV, developed the wide screen and the three-hour epic, moving out into country where its rivals could not follow it, so concert promoters will tempt us with large-scale works demanding total involvement of a sort we can rarely achieve in home listening. More and more, we go to the concert hall to be exalted, taken out of ourselves by listening to major masterpieces. It is perhaps also significant that there are more concerts than ever which include a visual or theatrical element. At the popular end of the spectrum, there are spectacular Tchaikovsky and Beethoven concerts with two, three or four military bands and flashing cannon in *1812* or the 'Battle' Symphony, while the avant-garde are bringing music-theatre works into the concert hall.

And, finally, aleatoric music: unpredictable, unrepeatable, and therefore unrecordable, issues a challenge which the record can never, in the nature of things, take up. Indirectly, the music of chance may partly originate in reaction to a world music that went on endlessly repeating the same tightly programmed works. But I doubt if any aleatoric music has been deliberately written out of a desire to go one better than the record.

'What has been sought', wrote Carlos Chavez in the 1950s, 'is not how to make the best music for the radio, but the best means of making the radio transmit music which already exists.' Broadly speaking, the same is true of the serious composers of our own day, who, like those of the past, have very rarely allowed the nature of the medium (radio or recording) to influence them directly. A handful of advanced composers of the 1920s did indeed experiment in cutting music directly on to the disc and in varying the speed of the turntable in reproducing sounds. But most have continued to recognise the new media only in their roles as music's faithful servants. Those commissioned to write for radio continue to write concert-hall music—the only difference being that noted by Stravinsky: that where rehearsal time and funds have been abundantly available (as with West German radio commissions) the styles of the new music have tended to be correspondingly complex, as if to take advantage of the opportunities offered.

It is not easy to be specific about indirect influences. It is possibly no more than a curious coincidence that Milhaud's early polytonal polyrhythmic works came into being just at the time when listeners could first hear naïve diatonic tunes of a sort often used by Milhaud jammed together in similar fashion as a result of radio interference. More importantly, all who write with radio or record audiences even vaguely in mind must be unsettled by the thought of the new, unknown audience. Those commissioned to write concert works can hardly forget that, if their works are broadcast or recorded, they are likely to reach an audience a thousand times larger than the first immediate audience. A 'first concert performance' may for this reason be like a speech delivered by a politician at a Rotarians' dinner. Ostensibly the politician addresses the Rotarians; but inevitably he has in mind the thousands who will read his speech in the papers the next day, or hear it reported by radio. When contemporary music sounds to us anonymous or stylistically uncertain, it may well be because the composer is in fact writing for an anonymous audience of uncertain needs and capabilities.

Radio and recording have changed the ways in which music is distributed, making it possible for the composer to reach a huge audience with a single performance of his music. This may be as embarrassing for a composer as for a TV comedian. Because the whole public can be reached with a single transmission, material that would in the old days have lasted a lifetime becomes obsolete in a few weeks. All the more incentive, we might think, for the composer to strive to write *lasting* works that will stand up to many performances. But the sad truth is, that the overcrowding problem has been intensified by the existence of the electronic media which have made possible the resurrection of the music of all lands and all ages, so that no one any longer has time for repeated hearings of unproved works. Disagreeable as the thought may be, we seem to be moving into an age of instant masterpieces, where a few selected works endure, while most contemporary music vanishes, like a birthday cake, after one or two carefully timed appearances. Soon, serious composers may be forced to revert to eighteenth-century attitudes, functioning as cooks rather than architects, accepting the proposition that it may be as honourable and worthwhile to devote genius to providing a banquet for immediate consumption as to erecting a monument that will endure—possibly unnoticed and unregarded—for many centuries.

On the credit side, there is a great potential audience of intelligent, experienced, but often preoccupied listeners now waiting to be acted on, if only the composer can find the right way to open the conversation. The problem is a huge one. How can he, who knows through direct experience only the small groups of *cognoscenti* at contemporary music concerts, get in touch with his new potential public? Unless he is ready to discard many of the preconceptions and attitudes of the past century, it is hard to see how he will ever get through.

I am advancing on dangerous ground. The effects of radio and recording on composers and performers can be observed in their compositions and performances. But the radio listener or record-user remains a distant, hypothetical creature, while the effects music produces on him can only be inferred.

To begin with facts that no one will dispute. The electronic media have brought music to vast new audiences; we may deplore the fact that errand boys no longer whistle popular songs or that TV has taken the place of domestic music-making; yet there has been a great broadening of musical taste, and a desegregation of musics that once 'belonged' to one class alone. I've heard road sweepers, car-park attendants, taxi drivers, window cleaners, Chinese waiters, humming or whistling Vivaldi, Brandenburg concertos, Wagner, Kabalevsky, and Britten; economists, doctors, solicitors, and even classical musicians singing or playing ragtime, pop songs, sentimental ballads of a type that would have been unknown in upper-middle-class circles in our parents' youth, and which would have been kept from the ears of the children as obscene magazines were kept from their eyes.

Many serious musicians follow Constant Lambert in complaining of the 'appalling popularity' of music in the radio and record age, and say that no one listens properly today. It is true enough that the media have created a new class of casual listeners, who work, drive or wash up to music. But the improper uses of today may easily become the proper uses of tomorrow; music is becoming threaded into our lives in new ways, and new routes to understanding will in time be opened up by casual listening and by repeated and fragmentary overhearings of music.

Radio and recording have sharpened our ears to niceties in performance of which fifty years ago we would hardly have been aware, and have made it possible for the casual listener to have more experience of the way music sounds in live performance than all but the greatest experts of the past. In the 1900s only professional critics were in a position to draw comparisons between the different interpretations of (say) Richter, Nikisch and Henry Wood in familiar works. Such comparisons must have been as unsatisfying and inconclusive as poets' comparisons between the beauty of Helen of Troy or Cleopatra and their own adored Chloes. But today anyone can make precise and specific statements about the first violins' phrasing of the third bar after C or the tuning of the timpani octaves. Recording has made less acceptable ideas of 'ideal' performance; instead, we have a broader concept of 'truth' lying somewhere between a theoretically infinite number of possible interpretations.

The parallel with photography (and particularly cinematography) is close. Photography destroys some of the mystery that surrounds the object, and particularly the mysteries of objects in motion. Eighteenth-century painters had their 'ideal' stereotyped images for galloping horses: forelegs pointing almost horizontally forward, rear legs horizontally back. Photography revealed less elegant but much more varied images of action, and effectively changed our view of nature.

Radio and recording have played a large part in weaning us from the 'black-and-white' morality which holds that the meaning of music is mainly embodied in pitch and rhythm; timbre, orchestration, refinements of articulation and phrasing being the extras. (For Vaughan Williams as for Brahms, orchestral music had to make sense in piano reduction to be accepted as valid.) Berlioz and Liszt were the forerunners, Debussy, Mahler and Delius the children, of the recording age: composers who worked in timbres and textures rather than in abstract melodies and harmonies.

Here too there is a parallel with the visual arts; it is not so long since, as Kenneth Clark writes, 'colour was considered immoral, because it is an immediate sensation and makes its effect independent of those ordered sensations which are the basis of morality'. We can only guess how music sounded to those who thought of instrumentation as one of the superficial trimmings of music. Such an attitude made acceptable practically any sort of arrangement and allowed composers much latitude in issuing their own music for clarinet *or* viola (Brahms sonata), violin *or* cello (Franck sonata). Did the arrangement of Strauss's *Till Eulenspiegel* for a salon orchestra of thirteen once sound like 'the real thing'? Even critics displayed what seems to us an extraordinary innocence when they wrote of instrumental timbres.*

But today, we can all be connoisseurs, discovering tastes, and shades of taste, which we never knew existed. New distribution methods have hastened the end of old-fashioned regionalism and nationalism, substituting a jazzy, kaleidoscopic jumble-sale

* George Pioch, describing the first performance of Stravinsky's *Rite of Spring*, wrote in 1913: 'You hear the prelude, where a wind instrument is dominant. We ask each other, which instrument can produce such sounds? I reply "this is an oboe". But my neighbour to the right, who is a great composer, assures me that it is a muted trumpet. My neighbour to the left, no less learned in music, opines: "I would rather think that it is a clarinet." During the intermission we ask the conductor himself, and we learn that it was the bassoon that put us in such doubt.' (Quoted in Slominsky, *Lexicon of Musical Invective*.)

atmosphere in which *anything* can come from *anywhere*,* and breeding a new race of omnivorous listeners, who take everything that comes their way, from Vittoria motets to Stockhausen's *Hymnen*, often passing it through their systems without digesting or absorbing the more nourishing ingredients. For in the electronic age of constant exposure to music, we do not necessarily grow out of styles and idioms: that is to say, exhaust them. We may only grow tired of them before we have grown into them. Yet the age breeds too, passionate specialists: people who have come by chance to discover the great love of their life. Fifty years ago, we could have gone to a concert every night of the year and never heard a note of Hotteterre, Quantz, Hummel, Alkan, Ives or Havergal Brian. Today, every music-lover has the chance to find his ideal and necessary companion through life, and the Donizetti Societies, the John Field Societies, and Arnold Bax Societies knit enthusiasts together into select communities of like thinkers.

*New sounds*

The function of the commercial record is to act as the faithful shadow of the live performer, moving only when he moves. But in other areas we have long been used to the idea of mechanical musics of many sorts each with a character of its own. Musical boxes, orchestrions, player-pianos, mechanical carillons can be appreciated in their own right. Primitive phonographs and gramophones now seem to us to produce a music *sui generis*; and I imagine that survivors of a past age who danced, in the 1920s, to records of Jack Payne or Debroy Somers played on portables with steel needles would feel that the atmosphere of the nostalgic past was lost if they heard the same music in hi-fi recordings played on the latest music system.

We allow ourselves to be entertained and touched by musical boxes and fair organs, because we feel they are doing their limited best to make real music—we listen to them as we listen to our children trying to pronounce difficult words in what we have decided is the proper way. But we would feel rather differently if the children began deliberately guying and

* This mixing of cultural elements is a characteristic of the age. In Caerphilly in Wales, you can still buy Caerphilly cheese and dolls in Welsh national costume. But the cheese is processed and packaged in a London suburb, the dolls come from Hong Kong.

caricaturing our speech, or insisted in talking in some language of uncouth sounds that made no sense to us.

This is one of the reasons why electronic music, in its early days, shocked and affronted so many traditionalists. And it was also a reason why the new medium appealed to many rebellious spirits. Their desire to move off into new territory: *not* to use the means at hand, to separate themselves from the main body of conformists, was very strong. The second main reason why the idea of electronic music offended traditionalists and appealed to revolutionaries was of course that it dispensed with the human intermediary. Some thought of this as a dehumanising process which the spirit of music would never survive. To others, it represented liberation; at last the composer could go his own way, freed from the tiresome, unreliable companion to whom he had been tied for so long. He could speak to his audience direct and dispense with the performer-interpreter.

We should not be too much impressed by the foresight of those who, earlier in the century, looked forward to the development of a totally mechanical music. At the tail end of the romantic age, composers chafed at all restrictions, and most of their prophecies were of the 'wouldn't it be nice if...?' variety. 'The full flowering of music is frustrated by our instruments,' wrote Busoni. 'The future is with the completely mechanical orchestra,' wrote Honegger, '... alone capable of solving the problems created by the growing demands of human interpreters.' But the prophets had no more power to bring about changes than Jules Verne had to construct the flying machines and submarines of which he wrote so eloquently. Percy Grainger, who boldly tried to construct his own music-making machines, spent the later years of his life conducting experiments which any engineer would have written off as impractical after a few hours' consideration. Yet the prophets were truly eloquent, and their poetic words, backed by their great reputations, induced a happy state of expectation among the radically-minded. The new age would be a golden age, of unimaginably precise effects and wonderful sounds. One prophet, Carlos Chavez—himself a considerable innovator—sounded a more realistic note: 'I should like to know whether the most mystically inclined man has ever heard "celestial music" that was not played on harps, flutes, and trumpets, or sung by voices.' But even traditionalists took seriously the claims of the visionaries, and prepared to rise to the defence of the precious composer-performer relationship, which suddenly became more precious in view of the new threat to its very existence.

When electronic music was at last born, in the 1950s, it did indeed make a great impact. 'The howls and clanks of this music' (Reginald Smith Brindle wrote in 1956) 'threaten our future. I admit the effect can be devastatingly dramatic, but it will fall into the wrong hands—those incapable of anything better.' Electronic music was discussed in the *Musical Times* in that year under the heading 'The Lunatic Fringe'. The radio playwright Henry Reed caused his avant-garde composeress Hilda Tablet to write *musique reinforced concrète*. Some of the earlier electronic works seemed to be leading us into worlds far removed from any we had entered before. We heard giants hammering with iron fists on the roof of the concert hall, or were whirled around in space as we listened to Stockhausen's *Gesang der Jünglinge* or other multi-track recordings. New kingdoms of sound waited for their Stravinskys or Weberns to divide and rule.

But as the dragon that was to destroy the old order came quickly closer, the traditionalists were relieved to see friendly smiles on several of its forty or fifty faces. In no time at all, even conventional composers were patting its head, and all the children at the conservatoires were clamouring for rides on its back. Academic disciplines have developed, composers have come to terms with the new music, often using it discreetly in the context of traditional works as a composing aid. There have been a few startling and revolutionary electronic works, and startling uses of electronics in mixed electronic-and-live music. New types of musicians have emerged, generally men and women whose imaginative powers are semi-mathematical, semi-musical. Many students take to electronic music because it offers them the chance to work systematically within a structured discipline, and many produce work which is interesting to initiates but no more revolutionary and no more designed to make an impact on the outside public than that early medieval music which is rightly labelled *Ars Subtilior*.

If this is a revolution, it is a delayed-action revolution, of which the musical community as a whole is not yet even aware. We are told to 'wait and see': 'Do not try to judge the potential of the man from the undisciplined cries of the infant. It is healthy, and it will thrive' (Tristram Cary). Enthusiasts insist that the revolution is with us already; Herbert Russcol writes, in *The Liberation of Sound*: 'For the young people who sense that ours is an age with a restless past, the non-personal sound of electronic music is *right* as the neurotic expressionist music of Schoenberg's *Pierrot Lunaire* and Berg's *Wozzeck* were *right* for the Vienna of half a century ago and as Aaron Copland's upbeat, affirmative Americana-in-music was right for America in the forties.' Russcol is far out in his reference to Schoenberg, who was ignored in Vienna by young and old alike in the 1920s; and equally at sea about the general impact of electronic music, which today has taken its place as one of the many genres of advanced (sometimes not-so-advanced) contemporary music which compete for public favour.

It is not difficult to understand why the new medium should fascinate so many traditionally trained composers. Use of the new medium allows the traditionally trained musician to view his own role objectively. He realises how vague are the specifications of even the most precise conventional notations, and how much, in the past, he has relied on the performer's traditional interpretative practices. Where before he has only specified pitches, durations, and pre-selected timbres, he now has to define his wants in precise and objective terms. Sophisticated and highly trained composers experience a sense of liberation when they are forced to adopt new modes of thought and to consider the nature of sounds *ab initio*. Often, they return as new men to more orthodox forms of music-making. Stockhausen, Berio, Babbitt and Cage have commuted between electronic studio and concert hall, taking with them to each valuable experience gained in the other.

But for the lay listener, electronic music remains a mainly esoteric and unknown art. Pure electronic music is, certainly, hard to listen to in the concert hall; not so much because it is 'inhuman'—there is really not much essential difference between a composer's use of tape and his use of an elaborate box of tricks such as the organ—as because of the difficulties of attending to sounds that can be referred to no familiar source. It is interesting to find how much easier it is to listen to Stockhausen's *Mikrophonie II* after we have had it explained to us in terms of the gongs and plastic beaters and brushes used to realise the work. Milton Babbitt has, indeed, suggested that it should be no harder to assimilate pure electronic music than recorded or broadcast music, which similarly comes to us out of nowhere and which can be referred to no visible sound-source. But it seems probable that even confirmed record and radio addicts place and assess sounds through their knowledge of instruments and voices, and that they would be disorientated if all reference-points were removed.

If music is tuneful, or structured in a reasonably familiar way, even this difficulty is easily overcome. No one has problems with the fun-sounds of television jingles or Moog-synthesised Bach, or with the electronic transformations of live sounds used by accessible composers such as George Crumb or Berio. The irony is, that even here the composers of functional and commercial music have got in ahead of the serious composers. It was in the worlds of radio, film, theatre and television that electronic music first found a world role. Millions of people who have never been inside a concert hall have been exposed to electronic spook-music, outer-space music, sophisticated orchestrations of pop tunes in which synthesisers and electric pianos play leading parts. In these areas, electronic music is already prosaically working for its living. And if the public ever comes to accept abstract electronic music in the concert hall, it will be partly as a result of its gradual acclimatisation through exposure to commercial entertainment music.

## *Death of silence*

The development of electrical recording has often been celebrated as the most important step on the path towards faithful reproduction. But to future generations it may well seem that the gift of decibels was more significant than the gifts of wide-frequency range and freedom from distortion. Before the development of the thermionic valve, recorded music had been a weakly and delicate child, kept at home and rarely taken out into public places. Much ingenuity had been used in attempts to increase its strength; the Auxetophone demonstrated at the Albert Hall before the First World War amplified natural vibrations by means of compressed air but was far too complex and delicate to enter the everyday world, while the acoustic gramophone could not compete with tea-shop orchestras, street pianos, theatre bands, or go on to the bandstands on the seafront and make its voice heard above winds and waves. Only when aided by microphones, amplifiers and (in due course) by magnetic tape, which made it possible to relay music for long periods without human intervention, could recorded sounds go out into the world to conquer or create new markets.

The battles of live versus mechanical music were as varied as the battles of the last World War. Sometimes huge armies faced each other in entrenched positions and for months no perceptible gains were made on either side (as in the theatres and restaurants where live musicians maintained their foothold till the 1950s). Elsewhere, a decisive breakthrough came after a short engagement (as in the cinemas). Sometimes, in the North African desert, armies advanced hundreds of miles in a day through country empty of enemy forces (in much the same way, piped music moved into railway stations, supermarkets, dentists' waiting rooms, and other places where music had never been heard before).

The war against recorded and piped music is fought on two fronts. The MU member who puts a *Keep Music Live* sticker on the back window of his car is thinking primarily of his job; but he is also quite likely to have an inbuilt objection to all indiscriminate uses of music that become possible when music can be broadcast from anywhere, to anywhere, stored up for future use and repeated *ad infinitum*. Serious musicians tend to think that all practical uses, even those that are socially acceptable, are irrelevant to their art. When Charles Burney was asked to name the 'uses of music', the only use he could think of was, to raise money for charity. I suspect that his response was defensive—Burney knew quite well that music could be used to keep up the morale of troops and to keep them in step, for dancing, or to create a genial atmosphere at balls and routs; but he preferred to ignore these uses. And so today, musicians won't consider very seriously, from a musical point of view, therapeutic and hypnotic uses of music, the use of music in signals (ice-cream carts and doorbell chimes), as a sedative for air travellers or a stimulant for office workers. They suspect, generally rightly, that people who use music for secondary purposes are little concerned with the music itself except as a means to an end. They note that the most distinguished therapists make use of music which seems to them to have no quality as music; that the driver of the ice-cream van happily cuts off 'The Bluebells of Scotland' in mid-phrase. Sacred objects are used for profane purposes—a point that was made back in the 1930s by the cartoonist Reinganum, when he showed Christmas revellers playing musical chairs as the

BBC Orchestra relayed a Beethoven symphony from the studio.

And most of all, they object to the indiscriminate use of recorded and piped background music. Every musician has a few good stories concerning its uses and particularly its abuses. We hear of the aeroplane music tapes played backwards without anyone noticing; of *Liebestod* at Niagara Falls or on Paddington Station; of sequences of third-rate tunes repeated at twenty-minute intervals in restaurant or waiting-room, the tune we disliked at first becoming even more dislikeable third time round. Musicians proclaim that great music is devalued by misuse; that precious silence is polluted; that the public are fobbed off with shoddy goods when they might be enjoying worthwhile music—or, alternatively, that the senses are so dulled by continuous music that listeners become psychologically deaf to all music, good and bad alike.

Music sociologists, generally serious-minded men, tend to fan such fears, and generally pick on the least desirable uses of music and quote the most extravagant claims of advertisers—who often lay themselves open to criticism and ridicule. An Indian Minister of Agriculture is quoted as saying that rice fields yield from 22 per cent to 58 per cent more when music is played to them (if true, why isn't music played to all rice fields?). We read of the Australian race horse Moozak who was restless and off his feed till Muzak was installed in his stable and of the specialised programmes offered by American background-music firms: 'Trust account music—music to bank by' and 'Music to strip by'. We are told that typists attain high speeds on jazz and dirges, but that jazz also increases the rate of error, or that British Muzak tends to rule out music with lyrics because workers stop to write them down if they enjoy them. Scraps of unrelated information suggest that the whole background-music scene is a bad, though slightly sinister joke.

The joke is sinister, because of the suspicion that we are being conditioned. If Muzak affects rice fields and race horses, what might it not do to humans exposed to it day and night? But research findings and later developments in the background-music industry suggest that the picture is not really so frightening. The publicity men have only themselves to blame if they have suggested that music is a more powerful and specific force than it really is, at least in its present uses.

The experiments on which planned music programmes for workers have been mainly based were carried out by the British industrial psychologists S. Wyatt and J. N. Langdon in the 1930s and by the U.S. Army's Human Engineering Department in the 1960s. They confirmed facts known to every composer: that music maintains alertness best when the type of music is varied; that continuous music is less effective than music interspersed with silences; that if music is liked it has good effects on the morale. Britain's biggest and most reputable planned-music firm, the British Muzak Corporation, sells a continuous stream of what are virtually little symphonies—fifteen-minute segments of sound and silence, made up each of five prefabricated units. A 'stimulus curve' is built into each segment, and into the day's programme (one aim being to counteract the effects of mid-morning and mid-afternoon low peaks). The stimulus rating is arrived at by applying a formula involving tempo, rhythm, instrumentation and number of instruments—a fairly crude measure of musical effect, but not an unrealistic one.

The idea of using music to manipulate men and women as if they were battery hens is odious to musicians—and also to factory workers who have increasingly rebelled against the idea of manipulation by management, and increasingly demand to be entertained with the sort of music they want to hear. Today, an almost up-to-date repertory is demanded and supplied. There has been a swing away from American light music, which was popular in the '50s and '60s; all countries are using more of their national music. At the same time, there are wider possibilities for free choice. Restaurants, hotels, supermarkets and airports, can belong to a cartridge library, and choose their own music programme. If you open a Japanese restaurant, Muzak will devise a special programme for you; but they would not be lined up to service a Restaurant Stravinsky, and generally steer clear of classical music because 'the dynamic range is too great'.

It seems, then that the trend is away from anonymous music discreetly tailored for background use towards more specific and positive sorts of music, and that long exposure does not beget indifference to music. It is true that commercially supplied programmes do not reflect serious music-lovers' tastes; background services evolved as a light-music industry, and nearly all the professionals involved come from that side of the fence. But as we know today, in the field of do-it-yourself background music any type—from crumhorns to Steve Reich—may be pressed into service. Remembering the way in which the record industry developed—in the first place purveying cross-talk acts, whistling solos and sentimental ballads—it seems probable that the background-music suppliers will come in time to discover and exploit the quality market.

I don't think we need be too much horrified by this prospect. Great music is robust, and survives misrepresentation. What harm was done to Beethoven by the innumerable 'Gems from Beethoven' the brass bands and light orchestras used to play? Record and radio have changed many things, but have not numbed our senses, as many predicted they would; nor do I think that background music will diminish our responses to interesting music. Certainly many listeners have become hooked on Brahms, Beethoven or Steve Reich through casual over-hearings on the radio, and I can imagine the same sort of thing could happen if commercial background music abandoned its cautious policy of providing little but mild musical pap. But we do need new sorts of work to meet the needs of a medium in which normal time-structuring cannot be effectively used, and in which the listener must be enabled to pick up the thread (if there is a thread) at any moment. Certain sorts of aleatoric and static, atmospheric contemporary music have possibly evolved partly in response to these new listening contexts. In the electronic age, *intelligent* casual listening is a possibility to be reckoned with.

One great objection to background music remains: that it pollutes silence, forcing us to listen to music we never asked for, and don't want, at all hours and seasons. Perhaps we preserve an over-rosy picture of the old pre-electronic world. The taste for silence is, I imagine, as recent as the taste for solitude. In the primeval cell, there is no stillness but a rushing flux of electrical discharges. In primitive societies, silence implies hostility. The country should not be silent, though crop-sprayers and hedge-cutters may reduce it to silence. Yet today we are sophisticated, and value silence all the more because it is hard to come by. The electronic media have put terrible weapons in the hands of the irresponsible—every man now has the power to make the loudest noises with the least expense of effort.

Though there will always be friction between the young, who like their music loud, and the middle-aged, who don't, I believe that there is less friction and less cause for distress than there was ten or fifteen years ago. The transistor is no longer a new toy; it is no longer obligatory for every holiday-maker to carry his own music around with him. Restaurants and supermarkets seem to be using their amplification systems with more discretion. And I suspect that musicians, ever skilful at following through a single line in a complex counterpoint, have learned increasingly to shut off and not to listen to what they don't want to hear. We seem to be toughened by experience, as those who live under the flight-paths near Heathrow are toughened—unless they become so hypersensitive that even the rumour of a distant Boeing drives them mad with anger and frustration. For a psychological element is involved. The visually-aligned man who lives in a tastefully decorated room is not generally upset by the packets of cornflakes on the table or the soapflakes by the sink. He has learned to *except* from the visual context. So too, in the new auditory environment, musicians are showing themselves flexible and adaptable; taking what they want, ignoring what they don't want.

# IV

## WORLDS APART

Since the 1960s, McLuhan and other prophets of the electronic age have been proclaiming that at last the barriers have gone down and we have become truly members of one another; 'Plurality of time succeeds uniformity of time'; old cultures are fragmented, and are succeeded by mosaic cultures. Those in the world of music can find plenty of evidence to support this view. Instead of making sustaining meals of concertos and symphonies, at fixed hours and in appointed places, we feed at any time of day or night on finely chopped polycultural salad; Lassus and Polynesian folk music, Beethoven and Berio rub shoulders as we pluck music from the air. Pop singers base their numbers on Indian ragas; the latest hits spread like a contagion through the world, so that African tribesmen hum the new pop tunes only a few weeks after their release in New York. Vivaldi concertos leap to no. 17 in the top twenty; Strauss, Mahler and Ligeti become known to millions through their involuntary contributions to film scores.

Yet in spite of all, there are still many smaller, isolated musical worlds, preserving their own standards and practices, and often their own repertoires, which have been hardly affected by the cultural revolution. (As Cyril Connolly once remarked, the intellectuals tend to be right about the direction of events but wrong about their timing; they consistently underestimate the world's resistance to change.) A large part of the population continues, in time of revolution, to go on as it has always gone on. Civil servants, gas maintenance men, and sewer men are not purged in times of crisis.* In music too, it is the *functionaries* —dealers in music that serves specific purposes—who are least affected by changes in the outside world.

The view of the various areas of functional music from the mountain-tops of serious music is one of uniform flatness. Those who live up in the heights are not in a position to see the gentle

---

* When, in 1942, Menuhin asked his Moscow hosts if anyone had done the same job in Russia for fifty years, they quickly found one in the hotel he was staying in: the hotel's lift man.

bumps and hollows that appear to the lowlanders as sizeable hills and valleys. They share a bland belief that life at the top is the only sort of life worth living, and show no wish to discover more about their neighbours below. This is all the more surprising when we live in an artistically broad-minded age, taking a respectful interest in the folk musics of distant lands, no longer in an arrogant missionary spirit seeking always to impose our own culture on others. We also have some respect for the more intellectual sorts of jazz, and for the separatist movements of the avant-garde.

The serious musician can tolerate all these kinds of music precisely because they are separate from his own music, and offer no threat to his own integrity. But in the worlds of church music, band music, and light-entertainment music, he is ill at ease because he is so nearly at home there. He is uncomfortable with church music because it is too tasteful; with band music, because it is not tasteful at all. They are near relatives who perpetually remind him of what he might have become; perhaps, even, of what he would subconsciously still like to become.

Yet the performers and listeners who inhabit these worlds are by no means musical morons and ignoramuses, but are often able and intelligent people; if they practise their arts with passionate enthusiasm, it is because they discover in them rewards of which the serious musician has little idea. His lack of understanding stems from his reluctance to think or talk about music except in abstract terms; but it would be as pointless to write of church or brass-band music in the abstract as it would be to describe a carpenter's skills and tools without mentioning the work he achieves with their help. That is why, in discussing functional musics, we must take a new viewpoint, and ask, not 'what is good music?' but 'what is music good for?'

*Church music*
A Marxist might claim that music was subjected to political misuse when employed to give a seductive taste to the opiate of the people: religion. But even the strictest musical moralists don't hold that music is demeaned by being put to use in the service of the Church. Western music grew up within the Church, and could hardly disown its mother and father. Church music is free of the taint of commercialism, and freer

than concert music of any suspicion of exhibitionism; since (in theory at least) even professional church musicians and composers do their work for the glory of God, or to affirm and strengthen the spirit of the community. The audience has receded to the point of infinity, so that music can soar aloft freely, no longer fettered by the need to stay within the limits of human understanding.

In practice, things are never so simple. Go to King's Chapel and listen to Lassus and Byrd, and the music does indeed soar aloft and is indeed glorious. Yet one understands the viewpoint of those who complain that evensong is no more than a concert in disguise. Music seems to be celebrating its own glory, which is fine for musicians. On the other hand, if we visit the church down the road where the whole congregation is singing, with genuine fervour and passion, our least favourite Dykes hymn, that is all right for the congregation but bad for musicians—and, the purist would add, 'bad for music'. In looking at church music, we are always subject to double vision: good is *bad* if it causes the congregation to fall apart in consternation—or possibly if it is so good that (as in King's Chapel) it draws in an audience of connoisseurs and musical agnostics. Bad music is *good* if it fosters community spirit in the congregation and raises it collectively to higher spiritual levels.

Today, the musician cannot dodge this issue. We have learned, again largely in theory, to be tolerant of other people's faiths and other people's musics. It would be impossible now to write a lengthy essay on church music, as W. H. Hadow did in the 1920s, giving a rapid outline of its evolution, referring to the parallel evolutions of Jewish, Catholic and Anglican music; bypassing altogether the Methodists, the Salvation Army, and all other sects that prefer the more questionable sorts of church music, and reaching the decision that a council of 'those best fitted to speak in the name of Church music' (ministers and musicians) should fix the critical standard and enforce the rigorous exclusion of all that fell below it. The watchword was to be: 'When in doubt, exclude.' Yet Hadow was a liberal man, widely read, and sometimes humorous. It was just that he knew precisely what was good and what was bad, in morals and in music, and that fortunately the boundaries exactly coincided.

Today, we accept the need for moveable boundaries and for tolerance; college chapels are good because they preserve the great traditions of church music, but Victorian hymns are good for those who like Victorian hymns. We acknowledge the existence of salvationists, and don't suggest that they would be better off singing Tallis. Church-musical society is in fact a microcosm of the society of the larger musical world; the great tradition persists, but innumerable deviant traditions (even within the Anglican Church) are now allowed to exist alongside. I say 'allowed', because the real-life situation has changed less than our assessment of it. The main difference is that we now acknowledge, and even welcome, the truth that the position of the boundaries between good and bad vary with the position of the viewer.

I would be treading on very dangerous ground if, as an agnostic, I tried to relate the musics of the various faiths, denominations and congregations to the faiths themselves. Yet the connection is very close, and expresses itself unambiguously to one alert to musical tones of voice. As Sir James Frazer wrote: 'Every faith has its appropriate music, and the difference between the creeds might also be expressed in musical notation.' A study of the musics of different churches could serve as a precise indicator to leaders of ecumenical movements, suggesting which groups were ripe for union and which would resist union like similar magnetic poles.

Of course, the community within a single church is not necessarily united in music and by music. For in the church, as in the world without, there is a rift between the amateurs—who want to advance deliberately, or not to advance at all—and the professionals, who are sensitive to a greater or lesser extent to winds of change. Professional church musicians are regarded as conservatives by fellow-musicians outside the church. But to congregations, and often to clergy, they can appear as dangerous avant-gardists, or as antiquarians perversely trying to put back the clock and return to plainsong or outmoded sixteenth-century motets.

The organist occupies an isolated position, both in the organ loft and as the one professional in a community of amateurs. He is also separated, by character and outlook, from fellow-professionals. He is the last of the guild musicians, highly trained experts who jealously guard the standards of their craft. The reports of examinations conducted by organists' associations are full of criticisms of Beckmesser-like savagery, which make the words of the average music critic seem mildness itself by comparison.* The emphasis on not doing the wrong thing is strong; the implication is that there is a right way (perhaps one and only one right way) to behave.

The profession forms, or attracts to it, those with an inbuilt respect for convention and tradition. It also attracts, or selects, those with particular sorts of manual and pedal skills, and formidable powers of coordination. Mere one-line players gasp in wonder as the organist expounds a five-part fugue, hands and feet flying in every direction. Nor is he a mere go-between; he improvises on his own account, fluently and in a number of styles and idioms, in the course of his everyday duties.

The organist rules as a viceroy in the kingdom of the church. If he fulfils all the roles open to him, he is a performer; a teacher and inspirer; a community leader and organiser of choir outings and cricket matches; a master-planner who ensures that music plays a creative part in enhancing the drama of ritual worship, without ever overstepping the fine dividing line that separates ritual drama from entertainment. Yet if he has the single-mindedness of many serious professionals, he is likely to develop schizophrenia. He must submit to the authority of clergy who may or may not understand or sympathise with his musical aims and ideals, and often becomes a subtle strategist who advances the cause of music by devious means. Like the eighteenth-century court composer, he must make the best of human material available. Choir boys' voices break just as he has shaped them into the semblance of musicians; older singers stay with him when he wishes they would depart. He fights against the sentimental hymns and anthems he detests, and which his congregation loves, knowing that he will never win the last battle. For in the last analysis, the music the congregation regards as its own has become an integral part of its identity, and that identity must be respected.

Though in his distant organ loft he often finds it necessary to anticipate the choir's entries, the organist lags a little behind the world-beat. Organists read organists' magazines, go to organists' conferences, and play their own repertory. What do other musicians know of Guilmant, Rheinberger, Widor and Reubke?

* 'Harmony weak, disregarding elementary rules ... workings undistinguished and drab ... ungainly spacing and excessive compass ... tonal answer was wrong and the inversion of the counter-subject was ignored ... phrasing haphazard and inconsistent' (from published examination reports of the Royal College of Organists, London).

Until fairly lately, the organist was free to range widely outside the church-music repertory in choosing recital pieces (symphony movements, overtures, and arrangements of instrumental and vocal solos once formed the staple recital diet). Earlier still, before the days of recording, the organ provided a satisfying orchestra substitute, and every great city supported a town-hall organist who reproduced much of the orchestral repertory loudly and impressively to the general satisfaction. But today, in our zeal for faithful performance, we frown on all arrangements, and the organist's activities are further curtailed.

Many church organists follow their vocation with single-minded devotion; others become organists because they possess the necessary talents and because the job offers a modest but secure living and a recognised place in society. Such men have no particular preference for sacred rather than profane music. When, in the inter-war years, the demand for cinema organists became brisk, many sedate church musicians moved into the new area and scored conspicuous successes there. The speed with which they took on new characters suggests, not so much a cynical abandoning of devout attitudes, as the existence of a real need to compensate for a certain blankness in their professional lives. The devils banished in church came trooping back in the cinema.

But the chief occupational hazard of the organist is not that he will break out and cause a scandal, but that he will become too comfortably set in his ways. To perform the same sort of music, with the same collaborators, at the same hour of the day, week after week, tends to dull the sensibilities, whether the locale is the theatre pit or the choir stalls and organ loft of a great cathedral.

In suggesting that the ritual, repetitive nature of the church musician's daily routine creates certain difficulties for him as a professional craftsman, I do not want to imply that ritual, repetitive performances are of doubtful religious or social value. As Benjamin Lee Whorf wrote, in describing the ritual music of the Hopi Indians: 'Unvarying repetition is not wasted but accumulated. It is storing up an invisible charge that holds over into later events.' Why should we condemn an Anglican congregation that holds fast to its favourite hymns and anthems more than the Hopi Indians for repeating the ritual performances handed down to them by their forefathers?

Leaving aside the moral question, I would suggest that there is a particular musical reason why music that has been used regularly as part of the church's ritual and in which the congregation takes part acquires a special sort of sanctity and rightness. To formulate a general principle: the strength of a congregation's attachment to music is directly proportional to its own active involvement in the performance. Congregations will suffer almost any sort of canticle or anthem as long as they are not themselves taking part; but the introduction of new hymns is quite another matter. The act of singing imprints music on the mind and in the affections. For the same reason, Salvation Army musicians and members of brass bands have stuck to their own types of repertory over the years, and have resisted attempts to educate them in the ways serious musicians think they should go. I believe my principle also partly explains the general conservatism of orchestral players, and the curious fact that many of the most daring reformers of the musical language—Berlioz, Wagner, Schoenberg among them—have been almost without the practical expertise in performance which might have attached them (physically and psychologically) to certain styles and techniques.

From a musical point of view, there is no doubt at all that we do right to preserve the great church music of the past and to perform it as well as it can possibly be performed. We will never again produce music that is so untouched by the world, so free from exhibitionist traits: religious-religious rather than secular-religious music, as Stravinsky described it, comparing church music 'from Hucbald to Haydn' to that of the nineteenth century: 'the latter inspired by humanity in general, by *Übermensch*, by goodness, by goodness knows what.'

But the existence of the great repertory does not help the contemporary composer of liturgical music, whose work, like that of the church restorer, must blend harmoniously with the ancient fabric. There are, of course, other reasons why he should be generally unable to write with ease and conviction for the church. The ethos of the age unfits him for anonymous service; his teachers have encouraged him to be himself; they have tenderly nourished his diffident, budding individuality and have only spoken the word 'derivative' in tones of disapproval. In the world of serious music, he may not even borrow from himself or re-till old ground without being blamed for it. But in church music, free and uninhibited expression of individuality is the last thing that is wanted. The composer exceeds his duties if he shocks, disturbs, or demands too much attention from his captive audience. For the composer who comes in from the outer world of music, the change of attitude required is so great that he can only achieve it by stepping out of his real character. That is why so much of the new music of the church is provided by competent and practical craftsmen who have not much character at all. Anglican church music of today too often seems to be stepping carefully, avoiding bad taste, avoiding unhealthy displays of emotion. It rejoices in diatonic discords, steers clear of chromaticism and expressive uses of the milder dominant and diminished sevenths that would remind us of nineteenth-century church music. There may be a hint of Vaughan Williams or Holst, but any suggestion of more recent idioms is still comparatively rare.

Yet even if there are few diminished sevenths to be found in today's anthems and hymns, we have become more tolerant of our forefathers' lapses of taste. We can allow that, out of that great mass of mediocre material, a few gems emerged. Stainer's *Crucifixion* has been recorded more than once, and even reviewed by highbrow critics. Fashions change so fast that we may find young intellectuals revelling in the luscious harmonies of Dykes's hymns in the same spirit as they appreciate the art nouveau tiles round the font, at the same time as older church-goers are enjoying them—having never stopped enjoying them—in the spirit of their own uncomplicated youth. One of the most intriguing aspects of the present scene is the way in which the coils of the evolutionary spiral have become compressed and tangled, so that the élite often find themselves boarding the same bus as the naïve and uninformed.

*Brass bands*
The uses of music are manifold. In the 1920s, Catholic missionaries introduced brass bands in Papua to 'subdue the dangerous energy' of the Papuan headhunters. No doubt it was in the same spirit that the earliest aristocratic patrons of the brass-band movement arranged garden fêtes and competitive festivals for the bandsmen of the 1840s, and that factory owners subsidised works bands (as they still do). But the dynamic energy has always come from within the movement. A great love of music is fanned by the spirit of contest, and blown up into ardent and

all-consuming enthusiasm. The atmosphere at the Albert Hall on the last day of the National Championships makes the Proms seem, by comparison, quiet and subdued as a sleepy afternoon matinée on a hot June day. The audience have the sort of informed involvement one expects at football matches, but rarely finds in the concert hall. Serious musicians often urge bandsmen to broaden their interests; but it is precisely the narrowing and concentration of interest on these occasions that generates, through music, liberating passions of the sort that every music lover would like to experience.

Though a good part of the bands' repertoire is made up of transcriptions of orchestral music, and though the language of their own custom-made repertoire is unproblematical, the existence of the bands was for long almost ignored by serious musicians. The 1927 edition of Grove's great dictionary gave a dozen lines to brass bands, described as 'the smaller variety of the full military band, employed by cavalry when on mounted duty'. Neither Mellers's sociologically aligned *Man and his Music* nor Jacobs's *History of Western Music* so much as mention the bands. They rarely get a mention in the *Musical Times* or *Music and Musicians*. Nor, in the specialist music shops and libraries, will you find copies of the bandsmen's journals the *British Bandsman* and the *British Mouthpiece*.

Bandsmen have occupied their separate world for so long now that they have evolved their own customs, notations and language. To the conventional musician, the brass band score presents a strange appearance. All parts but the bass trombone are written in the treble clef, the biggest basses sounding an octave and a half below written pitch; this is because conductors are almost always bandsmen themselves, and because there is a tradition of versatility: it is not at all unusual for players to transfer from euphonium to cornet and vice versa. Even the terminology has gone its own way; instead of *ripieno* (literally, filling-in) parts, bandsmen write *repiano*.

Until the 1960s, bandsmen had their own pitch, nearly a semitone above orchestral pitch; they still have their own repertory. Geehl, Ord Hume and Rimmer are names known only in the band world. Percy Fletcher, a light-music composer of the 1920s, is the Berlioz of this world, his *Labour and Love* the most quoted work in the standard book on brass-band orchestration. There is a vast library of transcriptions, including overtures, selections, arias from forgotten operas. ('Lend me your

Aid' from Gounod's *Queen of Sheba* is still famous as a trombone solo) and novelty numbers dating back to the early years of the century.

Those of us who were brought up on Wagner, Liszt, Tchaikovsky, Strauss and Elgar cannot warm to the grandiloquent tone poems and overtures of the brass-band repertory, which derive so obviously from these masters. We can no more take them seriously than a painter of the higher culture can take seriously the quite competent oil paintings of horses, ships in full sail, or bowls of flowers on sale in every high street art shop. There is something intrinsically disagreeable to us about music that seems to be straining to move into a higher sphere of art than the one we have assigned it to. It is inevitable that we should have these attitudes, and also inevitable that to the bandsmen they should seem intolerably snobbish.

Serious musicians also look down on the cult of virtuosity. J. A. Westrup deplored 'the energy wasted on practising airs with variations [that] could be used more profitably learning how to play *Voi che sapete* or *An die Musik* . . . the *air varié* is an anachronism. No doubt it encourages virtuosity, but virtuosity is of far less importance than taste.'

But those who hold that virtuosity is less important than taste (whose taste?) are not on the brass-band wavelength. Virtuosity is not (in band terms) a matter of playing very fast, or of mastering double- and triple-tonguing. It includes the passion for good ensemble, all the subtleties of expressive solo playing to which Roberto Gerhard drew attention in his hymn of praise to British bands: 'The quality of sound, power of modulation, nimbleness of attack, elegance of cantabile phrasing. . . .' Critics from the concert hall rarely seem to open their ears at all to the real qualities of brass-band playing as Gerhard did. How strange that Morley Pegge, the musicologist and hornist, should have dismissed the bands for their 'deadly monotony of tone', without distinguishing between smooth euphoniums, sharp, sometimes acid, trombones, warmly rounded tenor horns, and sweet, fluent cornets!

It is equally hard for the serious musician to stomach the openly competitive nature of band music. Certainly, contests produce curious attitudes of mind in listeners and players. At an important final, you can sense the supporters of a band willing their soloists to take their top notes cleanly—and perhaps willing their rivals to miss them. But it is no more reasonable to suggest that those involved are missing the music because they are more interested in the outcome than to suggest that spectators at a tennis match are missing the finer points of play because they too are interested in the outcome. And why is it less 'musical' to play well for glory and a silver shield than to play well for money, as professionals do, or casually and sloppily for the fun of the thing, as unmotivated amateurs may play?

For the bandsmen, competitions are only part of a whole way of life, socially and musically as rich and varied as that of the amateur operatic societies. In the *British Bandsman* you will find accounts of attempts on the world record for continuous playing; of the making of a giant dock pudding to raise money for a Yorkshire Junior Band and to be eaten at a pudding-and-bacon breakfast. Bandsmen advertise to find a band they can join when on holiday. Where work and banding go together, the whole of a man's life may be spent in an environment where social, personal and musical preoccupations and interests are inextricably mixed together.

This close intertwining of work and play tempts the observer to draw sociological conclusions. The conservatism and the plain, understandable harmony of band music could be related to the wish to affirm the strength of ties binding the close-knit work or village group together, 'togetherness' being better expressed in homophonic than in contrapuntal music. Those characteristic and thrilling brass-band sounds, the sharp-edged attack and the massive crescendo, satisfyingly express the strength-through-unity of a working-class group.

But it is better to consider, more realistically, the practical circumstances that directed the bands along one particular course. They came into being as a result of a technological breakthrough early in the nineteenth century; the keyed cornopean and cornet-à-piston provided sufficiently loud, waterproof, and relatively easy upper melodic instruments which could be used in all-brass ensembles. The repertory, like all the popular music of the day, was predominantly harmonic; so that when in the 1840s the smooth-blending saxhorns were evolved (for military use) it was natural that the bands should adopt them. Thereafter the course of evolution was set. The character of the ensemble as well as natural conservatism held the bands to the same type of repertory; mainly popular and 'effective' because so much of their playing was undertaken either in public places or at contests. Isolation was not so much deliberate as the result of circumstances. The bands never rejected Hindemith, Stravinsky or Schoenberg, because they never came across their music.

Attempts to bridge the gap between the bands and the rest of the musical world have in the past come to little, largely because of the superior attitudes of the élite, who made little effort to understand the nature and attitudes of bandsmen, and who regarded themselves as missionaries called to raise the band to higher things. Most of the composers who were persuaded to try their hand at band music knew so little of the band's inner workings that their music had to be scored by specialists—imagine the scorn we would heap on the band composer who came up with an orchestral work he could not score himself! A few of these works from the inter-war years have survived—often more valued by straight musicians than by the bandsmen. Ord Hume, Percy Fletcher, Cyril Jenkins and a few others are still the classical composers of the band world.

Today, the pattern is changing. Thanks to record, radio, and most of all to television, the rest of the musical world knows something about the bands, and the bands know something about the rest of the world. The growth of the band movement in schools has brought in players who don't blench at the sight of a $\frac{5}{4}$ or $\frac{7}{4}$ time signature. There is a new American-influenced light-music repertory, and many non-specialist composers are writing for the bands, not to elevate them to higher things, but because they love the sounds of brass and appreciate the bandsmen's special qualities. Arts councils give grants, bands appear at serious-music festivals, the publishers of superior music are building up brass-band catalogues.

But it seems unlikely that the old repertory of selections, *airs variés*, cornet duets and marches will be soon superseded. Such works are deeply embedded in the affections and life patterns of the band community; whatever their musical qualities, they form part of the ceremonials and rituals of their world. The musical life of the bands and of ourselves is all the richer because 'Life Divine' and 'Trumpeters Wild' are preserved—from free choice, not in an antiquarian spirit—alongside Elgar's *Severn Suite* and the latest works of Birtwistle and Bourgeois.

*Light music in decline*
The horrid words 'light music' remind us of a culture we would prefer to forget: that peculiarly West-European sort of entertainment music which was until lately intertwined with our higher art music, but which has declined so quickly that already conservationists are forming Light Music Societies to preserve whatever remains to be preserved.

The quiet, almost unnoticed death of light music is not in itself a particularly significant event; it can be seen as the inevitable end-result of a process that began at least as far back as Wagner, when art music began taking itself wholly seriously; and when, as a result, light-music composers began to be herded into separate compounds, and eventually to regard themselves too as animals of a separate species. But even if a patient has been ailing for years, his death brings about a flurry of uncertainty and readjustment among all who were ever near to him. There is an estate to be distributed, possessions to be shared out; though his living presence was resented, his death may cause awkward problems to those who are left behind. And so, though light music as a living, ongoing tradition has been booked for extinction for many years, its death has left a light-music-shaped hole in the heart of our culture; a hole in the heart, not as wide as a church door, but wide enough to affect the patient's character and performance. For light and serious music sprang from common roots. They served different audiences and different purposes, but their realms were interconnected, so that what happened on one was bound to affect the inhabitants of the other.

It is hard today to recapture the feel of the musical world before the barriers between light and serious music went up; as hard as to imagine the social life of the village community before the new motorway cut across it. Even in the 1920s, light music was still regarded as a genuine and necessary form of music, which a serious composer could write without demeaning himself. Many English composers made little distinction in style or manner between serious and light works. Much of the chamber music of lesser composers of the 1920s, including Bridge, Goossens and Cyril Scott, cannot be placed in any 'light' or 'serious' category. It would have been as acceptable at Wigmore Hall as in the broadcasts of the light-music sextets and septets which filled so many hours of radio time. Elgar's music of all periods is shot through with light-music influences, though often the original models are unknown to present-day listeners.* (Elgar's favourite closing formula of a *fortepiano* followed by rapid crescendo to sharp *sforzando* is a light-music cliché; possibly because it allows a ten- or twelve-piece salon orchestra to bring a piece to a clinching and impressive end.)

Light music is by nature ephemeral, and was never much discussed by critics, historians or dictionary makers. Yet up till the last war, a major part of the output of European radio stations consisted of light music. In England, the more serious sorts of light music were regularly played by symphony orchestras, and included in Proms programmes alongside the music of heavyweight contemporary composers. Serious musicians were ready enough to disparage light music for conventionality, superficiality, lack of intellectual or emotional content; but there was no question of disowning the younger brother who had failed to make the best of his chances. And when the second war came, the first precious possession that the BBC seized up in its flight from London was the Salon Orchestra, an ensemble formed from the finest players in the country (including Leon Goossens, Reginald Kell, Frederick Riddle and Anthony Pini), which was to uphold public morale by its superb interpretations of 'The Parade of the Tin Soldiers', 'The Donkey Serenade', 'Kitten on the Keys' and other masterpieces of the genre.

In fact, the BBC misjudged the situation. Classical and the more robust forms of popular music proved more effective than light music in sustaining morale, and the Salon Orchestra was disbanded in two years. But at least the point was made: that if light music is worth playing at all, it is worth playing well. Music for performance, whether of the eighteenth or twentieth centuries, demands sympathetic interpretation; which is partly why light music of the 1930s, casually played by *ad hoc* groups of the 1970s, sounds anaemic and faded as it would never have done in its day.

There are several obvious reasons why light music should have gone into decline in the post-war years. The home-grown

* Serious historians rarely acknowledge such influences. Henry Raynor, in his *Music and Society since 1815*, even makes the extraordinary statement: 'Light music is invariably a simplification of things current, or recently current, in other musical spheres.'

product has not been able to compete with livelier and more virile sorts of popular music, mostly imported from America. Radio and recording have broadened listeners' outlooks and made them intolerant of such mildly innocent entertainment. After the disappearance of the majority of cinema and restaurant orchestras in the 1930s, the root-source of professional light music had vanished, and with it many of the composers. Yet it is curious that the brass bands go on playing Heykens, Ketelbey and Haydn Wood as if nothing had changed; while even highbrows continue to listen to eighteenth-century or medieval popular music that, as far as solid contents go, is just as undemanding as Haydn Wood or Edward German.

Ultimately, one cannot be rational about these mysterious movements of public taste—or rather, of the taste of the small sector of the educated musical public which sets the standards for the rest of us. The tone of voice of a certain type of music becomes in certain periods insupportable; as the tone of voice of the late romantics was insupportable to many composers of the 1920s (Holst and Copland among them). In the post-war years, it became as *impossible* for a gifted student to compose undemanding entertainment music as it would have been for a student of the 1900s to compose polytonal fugues (like Ives, who was quickly pigeonholed as an *impossible* person doing *impossible* things). In the concert hall, music that speaks in the wrong tone of voice is equally unacceptable, while the BBC's Music Department has in the past few years totally separated itself from the dwindling Light-Music Division. Those with a talent for writing light entertainment music cross the barrier at their own risk. Malcolm Arnold, whose musicality and powers of invention are as great as almost any English composer of his generation, is continually reproached by critics for writing the music that it is in him to write.

Traditions of light entertainment music have always been more robust in Central and Southern Europe and in the Americas than in England, where we like to take serious things seriously, not presuming to smile at any of the 1,000 witticisms in Haydn symphonies, or at any of Beethoven's ribaldries except the most obvious of his bassoon jokes. Even our own light music has tended to the lugubrious—so many Monastery Gardens, Songs at Twilight, Sleepy Lagoons, and a notable lack of native equivalents for the furiant and tarantella. The high and serious tone of contemporary music just after the last war needed some alleviation; English music, as so often in the Victorian age, was suffering from an excess of good taste.

Fortunately for us, the elimination of the obvious and banal from serious music is never final. As in fairy stories the banished prince comes back, disguised, to conquer the land, so the necessary, life-giving baser ingredients of the total musical experience find their way back in disguised forms: as parody, as *faux*-naïveté, in dramatic contexts where the composer can put on a lewd or ribald mask, or, most fashionably, in collage.

All these forms of escape-from-seriousness are to be found in the advanced music of the '60s and '70s. And it is curious to find that, in reacting against the intellectuality and élitism of much mainstream contemporary music, the avant-garde seems to be recapitulating some of the attitudes and activities of the musical entertainers of fifty years ago. The stage bands of the '20s and '30s specialised in cross-talk acts, battles between pianists and percussionists, dramatically staged solo spots for xylophones and electric organs—all the ingredients of music-theatre were already present; while every night, jazz pianists and buskers were entertaining the public with what, if they had only known the word, they could have labelled as aleatoric music. And so the spiral turns again; and we find that we are back—at a somewhat higher level—at almost the point from which we set out.

## *Avant-garde*

Avant-gardism is always with us. From the beach, we watch wave after wave break with a fine flurry of spray and froth, and fear for the safety of our sand castles; the waves generally peter out into gentle ripples, without much affecting the steady and predictable rise and fall of tides. But in the 1960s we in England, a little late in the day as usual, became aware of a new and more purposeful wave of avant-garde activity, which even in its early manifestations produced perceptible changes in the tides and currents of our musical lives.

An artistic or musical avant-garde is rather more than an advanced guard, hastening on in front of the main body, which body will eventually catch it up and consolidate the gains it has made. It is a revolutionary party, anxious to put as large a distance as possible between itself and the army of traditionalists—including contemporary-art or -music traditionalists. In this, the new avant-garde of the '60s ran true to type. It protested, often spectacularly, against the intellectual severity and narrow specialism of concert-hall behaviour. Much energy and enthusiasm went into the development of new notations and new rules of play which would hand back responsibility to the performer. Influenced and often abetted by the pioneers of electronic music, the avant-garde pushed back the boundaries to include every sort of noise in the musical vocabulary; but even here there was a strong element of burlesque and parody. Key-rattling, puffing air through trombone mouthpieces, playing pianos with mallets and clothes brushes, from underneath or from within, sitting in silence for 4 minutes 33 seconds, are more than new modes of music-making. They are also protests against the smoothness and predictability of conventional performances and against the law which declares that traditional instruments shall only be played in traditional ways by traditionally trained performers. 'Away with the scale! Away with themes! Away with melody! To the devil with so-called "Musical" music!' the youthful Xenakis proclaimed.

It was not by chance that the wave broke just at this time. The new avant-garde represented the counter-force to the solidly-based and responsible contemporary-music establishment which came into being in the post-war years; funded by Arts Councils and radio stations; encouraged by sympathetic critics, its works discussed as seriously and long-windedly in the learned journals as those of the great masters of the past. At the same time, rigorous disciplines based on serial procedures were being introduced in universities and conservatoires, where composition teachers of the past had generally limited themselves to setting exercises 'in the style of' this or that composer of the past (back-seat driving with Bach or Beethoven), or gently encouraging the student to express himself in any way that would bring out his own individuality. From this time on, conscientious intellectually aligned students could put their noses to the academic grindstone as (they were told) the great composers of the past had done, and turn out genuinely 'contemporary' music, in the honest belief that, if they couldn't be great, they could at least be good craftsmen.

But universities breed visionaries as well as intellectuals, rebels as well as conformists. With the growth of the student population the number of rebels also grew. Early outbursts of avant-gardism had the generous inclusiveness of so many student movements. The barriers between the arts were to be taken down, hands were stretched out to the illiterate and unskilled, music was to take its place again as a political and social force in the lives of the whole community. The spirit of lunchtime theatre prevailed. We sat on hard seats or on the floor and listened to rough, enthusiastic, performances. Intervals stretched out endlessly while music stands were arranged in new ways to hold the giant avant-garde scores, or while the experts tried to trace the wiring fault in the amplification system. Clowning was encouraged; composers demonstrated sympathy with underprivileged instruments: percussion players, bass players and trombonists were the stars of many avant-garde events.

The avant-garde of the '60s had its folk heroes, Satie, Ives and Cowell among them, and its leaders among the older generation: Cage, Kagel, Feldman and Stockhausen among the most influential. But it was predominantly a youth movement, and drew in many non-musicians. Anyone who attended earlier lectures and concerts given in England by Cage or Stockhausen, or by pioneering native groups, got the impression that a whole new audience had suddenly appeared from nowhere: much necklaced and braceleted girls with bare feet, men in earrings and fringed leather jackets, arts students and engineering students as well as music students, queued up to get into the ICA or Elizabeth Hall, disconcerting even the most optimistic promoters, who had printed programmes enough for the usual sparse contemporary-music audience.

The movement did not fade away, but grew steadily in strength and momentum, becoming professionalised and commercialised in the process. One reason for this success was that avant-gardism recognised the need for the composer to make common cause with the performer, whose status and outlook had changed so much since the 1930s. Performers emerged who were delighted to accept the new responsibilities offered them in indeterminate music, and to enter into new relationships with their instruments. Playing on the wrong side of the bridge, experimenting with split or bent notes, conventionally trained players became children and amateurs again, and rediscovered the spirit of adventure in which they embarked on their first C major scale, never quite sure where the next note would come from or how it would sound when it did appear. Avant-gardism still appeals only to a minority of professionals;

but for those on the wavelength, it offers cathartic release from the monotony and sobriety of everyday concert life as well as a chance to collaborate in new discoveries.

Publishers (and not only Universal Editions) took to the new graphic scores with enthusiasm—here at last was a music that not only sounded different but looked different, while more flexible reproduction processes allowed them to print freak scores on circular plastic discs or with a new range of symbols for each new piece. Critics found that the new music of action made good copy. Whatever they thought of the sounds, they could write entertaining pieces about toy pianos played by model steam engines; or about competitive games for improvising orchestras in which the score is signalled in coloured lights; or about circus pieces like Kagel's delightful 'Two Man Band', in which earnest research students from German universities, sitting at the centre of a grand complex of remote-control wires, rods, treadles and keyboards, play for an hour on a strange assortment of musical and non-musical junk-shop material.

Kagel, Cage and Stockhausen, and first generation avant-garde performers such as Siegfried Palm and Vinco Globokar, were skilful publicists and entertainers; something that was very necessary in the 1960s. Their presence on the platform was often an essential part of the performance; some of the most dismal concerts have been those at which anonymous groups of players have tried to reproduce the works of these masters from the pretty scores which in fact tell so little about the magic generated by inspired prophets and clowns. Watching a respectable group of salaried musicians from a Scandinavian radio station conscientiously attempting an ambitious avant-garde programme, in the early 1970s, I remember feeling that avant-gardism had come of middle-age, none too gracefully, and that it was past the hour for the next revolution.

But after the age of protest and wild display, a more sober period of consolidation followed. Composer-performers such as Steve Reich, Heinz Holliger and Barry Guy came to the fore: specialised professionals, their arts as skilled and subtle as those of the virtuosi who spend their lives playing Mozart, Beethoven and Brahms. The intellectual element in avant-garde has grown stronger; often the dividing line between mainstream and revolutionary contemporary music vanishes altogether. Many avant-garde innovations have been accepted into the common idioms of contemporary music, so that we find the once outrageous techniques and sounds of the 1960s used freely in what are basically quite conventional works.

The more adventurous avant-gardists are still, as in the past, hampered by their lack of the expertise they need to carry out their ambitious plans. In mixed-media works there is often a great gap between the professionalism of musical performance and the amateurish acting, dancing, lighting or décor. Musicians who are not visually aligned or trained in theatre arts cannot transform themselves instantly into all-rounders. Devisers of new musical games forget that games which are amusing for the players are often very boring for the spectators. Avant-garde composers are curiously old-fashioned in treating notation as an 'engine of immortality', notating in laborious detail minute refinements of action which can only be successfully communicated *viva voce* or by example. Since the greatest quality of avant-garde music is its spontaneity, it would often be better to forget the message for posterity and concentrate on the living, evanescent performance. The composers' philosophical views tend to be as muddled as their mathematics. An almost mystical belief in the virtues of graphical notations as being 'psycho-visually correct' will not bear examination, and political beliefs in the free ensemble as a model of society do not excuse the extreme boringness of much free-for-all music.

Avant-garde music is by nature a break-away movement; yet it has never yet broken far away from the parent society. Avant-gardists have made themselves at home in our conventional concert halls. Like the rebellious children of staid middle-aged parents, they stay on in the family home while preaching revolution and disruption; there is room for all, and anyway they have nowhere else to go. The wildness of our musical rebels is acceptable to all concerned because we—and they—know that, however hard they huff and puff, the walls will not fall down. The English musical establishment, like the Catholic Church, has tolerance for its rebels and generally manages to minimise their destructive potential by accommodating them within the system. Moreover, we need our rebels: they open the windows and allow a much-needed wind of careless madness to blow through the stuffy, all-too-respectable mansion.

Already, the next wave has broken. There is a new generation of young composers, largely inspired by Reich and Riley, who are producing mathematically organised, highly systematic works which are generally lumped together under the heading 'experimental music'. Yet the avant-garde movement of the '60s has not yet spent its force. There is always the danger that we will classify as especially significant the movement that came to birth at a significant moment for us. But it seems to me that the '60s avant-garde may have special importance in the history of music. It recognised the changed status of composer and performer; it recognised the need for a music that could be enjoyed now, rather than (perhaps) in fifty years' time; it accepted the proposition that a splendid firework, which explodes once-for-always, could enter the realm of art-works together with the marble statues, deathless masterpieces of painting, literature and music, destined to last for ever and to take up space in the world and in our minds which no longer exists. It opened its ears to the sounds of the world and tried, for the first time in the history of the West, to incorporate them in its music.

# V

## THE PAST THROUGH THE EARS OF THE PRESENT

MOVEMENTS INTO A possible future and into an unknown past have one great thing in common. They are movements away from the central tradition into areas of discovery, in the course of which performers may find, not only a new repertory, but their lost souls. They are liberated by escaping into lands of strange timbres, released from the bondage of academic training which lays so much emphasis on the specialist techniques appropriate to nineteenth- and twentieth-century standard classics. They regain some of the responsibility taken away from them by composers of the last 200 years, and return to attitudes of innocence as they learn again to play on unsophisticated instruments, or (in avant-garde circles) treat their sophisticated instruments in unsophisticated ways. They become once more complete musicians.

*Early music*
In the early-music world, men of many talents still flourish. Players often make or restore their own instruments; they turn their hands to wind, strings and keyboard, like medieval town musicians or modern bandmasters. They diligently read the treatises on ornamentation or on sixteenth-century brass instrument embouchures. In this area the roads have not yet been tarred and metalled and signposted for traffic; every man needs to be his own guide and musicologist.

The very real delights and satisfactions of the early-music enthusiasts are not limited to appreciation of the music itself—even though without the promise of a rich, almost unknown repertory there would be no early-music movement. The element of rediscovery is often as important as the element of discovery. To play in a Brandenburg Concerto or a Telemann Sonata on a one-key baroque flute after having spent years of your life with the sophisticated Boehm instrument is to take to a bicycle after driving around for years in a closed saloon car. You rely on yourself more and on the instrument less. You can move less quickly (unless circumstances are very much in your favour) but you can still get, and give, an impression of amazing speed. You are more likely to come off when cornering; but remain in closer touch with the musical landscape through which you pass.

It is not really surprising that a good many performers should have seized the chance to escape from a system which demanded so much in the way of narrow, specialised study, often leading to a place at the back desks of a symphony orchestra. How many months does it take the violinist to learn to play fingered octaves in tune, and what is the artistic reward? The movement has also been given strength and intellectual weight by a new generation of university-trained scholar-performers, who have sometimes combined musicological know-how with high talent in presenting old music in living form. But the early-music revival would never have grown as it has if it had not also filled a need for audiences. When we are as much exposed to music as we are today, the need for a wider menu, for fresh sounds and fresh approaches, becomes acute. It is not that we grow out of the classics, but that from time to time we urgently need a change of musical air. Circumstances have also made us tolerant of all sorts of unfamiliar sounds and processes; medieval music no longer sounds uncouth to us, and the recorder no longer causes us to smile pityingly because it does not sound like a flute. And as performances become more expert and more idiomatic, it becomes easier to appreciate the many marvellous qualities of the forgotten repertoires of the past.

The process of popularisation has been speeded up by the record companies, who have caught on to the fact that there is a large audience for early music. With their help, Franz Bruggen and David Munrow soon became popular heroes, their poster-sized portraits in the window of every record shop. But big-business selling methods do not belong in this market, and I doubt whether such records as 'Popular Hits of Gregorian Chant' reached the right public—or any public at all. Early musicians are individualists, and early music remains a sort of cottage industry. Skimming through the advertisement pages of the successful magazine *Early Music*, you get the impression of a whole world of performers, instrument makers, editors and publishers busily at work in university towns, barns, mills and workshops all over Britain. Early music appeals to do-it-yourself instincts as strongly as does hi-fi. As many tempting extras are offered as in the motoring magazines: stools and chairs 'to complement your instrument'; special cherrywood *early-music* stands at 80 dollars apiece; kits with which to 'flower your own harpsichord' with authentic Ruckers bees, birds and flowers.

The passion for authenticity (which I shall be discussing at greater length in the next section) is a driving force in early-music activities. As record enthusiasts come to terms with music in comparing performances, so early-music enthusiasts take a firmer hold on their loved works when they can discuss them in terms of *notes inégales*, added appoggiaturas, or the conventions of *musica ficta*. Often it seems that detective interest is stronger than musical interest; the delight an expert has in deciphering an obscure notation will blind him to the fact that the music itself may seem surpassingly boring to the uninitiated (parallels with avant-garde games need hardly be stressed). But for those involved, the detective problems—and even the altercations with rival experts (for early-music men tend to be argumentative and intolerant)—add zest and meaning to the music. They are the $x$-factors which, in every context, make it possible for the music-lover to assimilate music so that it suffuses his whole being.

Both avant-garde and early-music communities originate in the coming together of enthusiasts with amateurs' enthusiasms and no particular longing for fame or money. Dolmetsch, the father-figure of early music, was often criticised for condoning amateurish performances and persisting in regarding ensemble music as the 'music of friends' rather than as public exhibition. It is still sometimes hinted that early-music performers have chosen a soft option, and would get nowhere in the world of conventional music; and sometimes such criticism is justified.

But often, such comparisons prove nothing; for new sorts of musicality are demanded both in avant-garde and in early music. It is no longer a relevant criticism of a viol player to say 'he was never a very good violinist' any more than it is relevant to say of an avant-garde composer, 'he could never tell the difference between a dominant and a diminished seventh when he was at the College of Music.' The ability to skim through Wieniawski studies or to discriminate between conventional harmonies may prove a hindrance in the new field of action. Those who have spent years learning to play very fast, very loud and very high on conventional stringed instruments have to unlearn much before they can begin to interpret old music convincingly. The avant-garde composer may think himself into new attitudes all the sooner if his mind is not rutted with the tracks of conventional thought-processes and modes of listening.

Early music generates its own forms of snobbery and élitism. The obligation to do the right thing in the right way can be carried to absurd lengths. First-rate cellists sit idly by while third-rate gamba players labour through the Bach Passion obbligatos. We suffer from premature experiments as at avant-garde concerts, when teams of cornettists play Gabrieli with the uncertain attack, intonation and dynamic control of mediocre schoolboy trumpeters. Inaudible harpsichords or lutes add nothing to our pleasure. Like the mutes who once walked in all well-conducted funeral processions, they are there because propriety demands their presence.

But we should not bother too much over the unsuccess of public performances of old music in big concert halls, in which it must often sound as out of place as Indian music sounds when transplanted into an alien environment. The early-music movement still draws its strength mainly from amateurs. It offers them the opportunity to join in a pioneering movement (when the difficulty of contemporary music and the attitudes of contemporary composers actively discourage them from pioneering in that direction). Amateurs are delighted to find that after a few weeks' study they can begin to make reasonably pleasant sounds and join in ensemble music, of which there is a large and expanding repertory. Amateurs and professionals are not separated by a whole exclusive professional training—there is still a sort of companionship in early music and a democratic sharing of pleasures and ideas. The mainly youthful audiences at early-music concerts are as distinctive and as unlike conventional audiences as avant-garde audiences once were, and are almost as knowledgeable as audiences at brass band festivals. As in the case of avant-garde activities, the new attitudes count for even more than the new-old music. They tell us reassuringly that the ancient tree of Western music is still thrusting out hopeful new green shoots.

*Authenticity*
In every period of rapid change, conservationists spring up to

guard the heritage of the past. As the bulldozers move in, we campaign to save Tudor mansions and condemned churches; and also industrial buildings, cast-iron bridges, Edwardian hotels, picture palaces of the 1920s. As the pace of progress accelerates, little-valued objects become period pieces almost while we watch. Vintage cars and bicycles are 'saved for the nation'; soon it will be the turn of the washing machine. the hair dryer, the plastic aeroplane cutlery.

The early-music specialists just described are the most fanatical conservationists in the world of music. But in the last forty years, a great change in the climate of opinion has affected all serious musicians. In the 1930s, Handel's oratorios were invariably given with Mozart's additional accompaniments or with Prout's added to Mozart's. His *Water Music* was only known (in England) in Harty's much-worked-up version with added clarinets and brass. Tovey, a great scholar and musician, had no qualms about publishing Haydn piano trios with cello parts rewritten to give a Brahmsian texture. Operas and even symphonies were often heavily cut. *Tristan* was put on at the Old Vic, home of English Opera, with an orchestra of nineteen and cut to two and a half hours. No one dreamed of performing Bach's Passions in German so as to savour the sounds of the original vowels and consonants, and we happily accepted the piano as a superior sort of harpsichord, not only for Bach continuos, but even in Scarlatti sonatas.

We order things differently today. Opera choruses learn Russian phonetically so that they can sing *Boris Godunov* in the original.\* Arrangements are *out;* it is barely admissible to give extracts from Wagner's operas in the concert hall. Operas are restored to their original uncut versions, and we never entertain the notion that a conductor or producer may even have improved an opera by cutting it. Symphonies are given complete or not at all, and we would not dream of cutting them as Beecham once cut Elgar's First Symphony (from 50 to 35 minutes). Where Mahler once eliminated all written-in appoggiaturas from Mozart's operas, we put in the unwritten ones that we think Mozart's singers might have added, and the cadential flourishes that virtuoso singers once indulged in on their own initiative. I remember my horror when, in the 1940s,

---

\* According to Ernst Roth, even Russians could not follow the words of the Covent Garden production of 1958.

I heard a French Sarastro drop down to a low E that was not in the score at the end of '*In diesen heil'gen Hallen*'. Today, I would smile approval.

Most serious musicians and lovers of serious music would today accept the two propositions: that music is likely to sound its best in authentic performance; and that we have a moral duty to follow a composer's directives as faithfully as we know how. The general truth of the first proposition is a matter of experience and common sense. When we hear works of the past stripped of inappropriate 'interpretative additions' and played on the instruments and with the forces they were written for, we hear them anew, often seeming to get the point for the first time. Who would ever want to return to hearing Elizabethan consort music played on modern strings rather than on viols, or Scarlatti sonatas on the piano? Even in precisely notated twentieth-century music, there may be great gains in going beyond the composer's directives in search of authentic style. Stravinsky merely stipulates 'bassoons' in his Octet—but how much better the work sounds with the French *Buffets* for which he originally wrote!

If we were to revert wholeheartedly to eighteenth-century attitudes, we would revert to a view of music as 'material for performance' and so attitudes of disrespect would in fact be 'authentic'. But our zeal for historically correct attitudes does not yet stretch that far; nor do we demand that orchestras break down in Beethoven symphonies because they used to do so in Beethoven's day. Yet there are times when we misrepresent music by playing it better than it should be played. According to Richter, Wagner expected the strings to go 'swooshing up and down' in the *Tannhauser* overture, only approximating to the written notes. The critic John Runciman suggested, in the 1890s, that such effects were deliberately planned by composers, and that we misrepresented them by playing with pedantic accuracy. The battle scene from Strauss's *Heldenleben* must have sounded a good deal wilder and more shocking when orchestras were barely coping with the written notes—'modern *because* badly played', to misquote Schoenberg.\* Watch the double basses in the Pastoral Symphony storm, and you will see that they are still sliding their whole hands up and down the strings making no attempt to play the written notes. If we trained a team of super-players to perform the parts

\* 'My music is not modern but badly played' (Arnold Schoenberg).

exactly as they are notated, the storm would certainly lose some of its wildness.

In practice, we can never hope to live up to the precepts of the more uncompromising advocates of work-fidelity. 'To understand Bach against the background of his time,' wrote Edwin Fischer, 'we must set aside all the music of Haydn, Mozart, Beethoven, the whole Romantic Movement, and also all the philosophy and free thought, the political conceptions and ideas, of a later generation.' But we cannot rid ourselves of twentieth-century knowledge and attitudes, and we would be the poorer if we did. Why should we not enjoy Mozart concertos played on Steinway grands, or Handel's concerti grossi played with modern techniques on modern instruments, as well as enjoying the authentic performances of specialist groups? One sort of interpretation throws light on the other, and both throw light on the music. Non-specialists may feel inclined to pity the fanatics, to whom the very idea of clarinets in Handel is upsetting. To the expert, an anachronism is shocking because it is an anachronism and no other reason is needed to reject a non-historical ornament. Even the sight of foot-pedals on a harpsichord upsets the purists—it is necessary, for the sake of authenticity, that the player shall experience all the original awkwardness of changing stops by hand. For the fanatic, there are as many bars to enjoyment in everyday performances of music of the past, as there are for the experts who cannot enjoy a western film because the cowboys ride their horses in twentieth-century style.

The doctrine of work-fidelity is not held in light- or popular-music circles, where there is no assumption that music exists in one true form, or that the composer necessarily knows best. Anyone can try his hand at arranging, provided he is prepared to pay the first composer his due royalty. Often, arrangements are artistically more worthwhile than unpolished originals, representing an artistic collaboration in which composers, arrangers and performers have all played a part. Serious composers operate to other rules; but that does not automatically place them on a higher moral level. Nor can we pretend to be more enlightened than eighteenth-century musicians because we treat with awe and respect music they treated with familiar disrespect.

There are a number of secondary reasons why the doctrines of authentic performance should have taken such firm hold in the minds of almost all straight musicians. The growing infiltration of university musicians into the performers' world has led to a wide acceptance of scholarly standards. To issue a corrupt text—or, by extension, a corrupt performance—is to commit a crime against scholarly morality. Radio and recording have refined our taste for timbres and textures, so that we no longer accept arrangements as rough equivalents for the real thing. The threat of commercialism, with its 'customer is always right' attitudes, leads defenders of the truth faith to hold all the more strongly to the doctrine 'the composer is always right'. Disorder and uncertainty in the outside world lead us to mistrust our own hunches; we appeal to history, to treatises, to the ur-text, which we study as minutely as biblical scholars study the sacred writings, and play every move according to authenticated precedents.

We may well agree that most music sounds better played the way it was written and on the instruments for which it was written; but it is harder to see why we have a moral duty to play it that way. The performer is never in the position of the architect or picture-restorer who can destroy the original fabric in the process of restoration (When Lord Grimethorpe had finished with St Albans Abbey, it was as though he had arranged Beethoven's Fifth Symphony for accordion band and destroyed all scores and recordings of the original in the process.) He can do no more harm to a work than the cook who varies one of Mrs Beeton's classical recipes; and in an age of multiple recordings, there is not the least chance that his 'misrepresentation' will have any long-term influence on world opinion. He may make a fool of himself, but he cannot make a fool of Beethoven. Why should he resign his rights to collaborate in the realisation? And why must we assume that because composers generally know best (and Beethoven will always know best) that minor composers will always know best? Or that we may not devise ways of varying older music just as interesting and appropriate to our own age as any originally contemplated?

And why should the composer acknowledge a moral duty far more strict than any recognised by the recreator of a famous ballet or the producer of a famous play? It is true that the directives of the musical score give more detailed instructions, so that the performer is allowed less initiative in the first place. But that does not explain the different standards of 'faithful performance' in drama and music—most tellingly illustrated in music-drama. Wagner wrote both words and music for his operas, and left detailed instructions for production and staging. To these, modern producers pay little attention. It causes the mildest of scandals when Siegfried wears modern evening dress, when the entry into Valhalla is played on a bare stage, or when the forge is replaced by a steam hammer. But if a conductor replaced the horns with saxophones, or strengthened the bass line with electric guitar, the earth would open and swallow him up.

As Jonathan Miller once observed: the performing arts (and music most of all) 'have been dogged by a sort of pedantic romanticism about the obligation we owe to the author of a work'. He added: 'Once it has left the originator's hands we owe him nothing at all.' But the root-cause of our passion for authenticity is emotional rather than rational. The great composers of the past are father-figures, who can do no wrong, and we abase ourselves before them. Great works become sacred works, and the impious wretch who adds a rhythm section to Mozart's G minor Symphony is guilty, not of a joke in doubtful taste, but of sacrilege. These attitudes are not to be reasoned about: they spell faith and commitment. I have not avoided talking about 'serious' music and 'serious' musicians in this book, because the word is the just one. We hang our faith on our belief in absolute musical truth; in masterpieces without blemish, in god-like master-composers. Such attitudes may not be at every point logically defensible; but they provide the framework within which the serious musician lives his life.

Even natural sceptics are swayed by this faith when they enter the inner citadels of music. We laugh at the absurdities of the fanatics, mad for authenticity at any price; at the inaudible harpsichords, out-of-tune cornetts, and endless exposition repeats, made because *they are there*. But I find that my own spine tingles with indignation when I hear Weingartner's re-composed brass parts in Beethoven's Choral symphony. And I observe that Jonathan Miller, once he gets inside the opera house, treats the music of Mozart and Tchaikovsky with as genuine and understanding a respect as any musicologist fresh from university.

### Cult of the masterpiece

Performers and listeners; professionals and amateurs; traditionalists and avant-gardists; international conductors, soloists and orchestral players; impresarios and managers of record companies; all agree on the absolute value of the masterpiece, whether it is the known masterpiece of the past or the possible masterpiece of the future. Its existence justifies the performer in his decision to devote his life to music. Through the masterpiece, he is able to discover his own nature more fully; entering into a world of ideal values, rising above himself to reveal to listeners wonders and mysteries of which, if it were not for him, they would know nothing.

The masterpiece (realised in the master-performance) holds within it the power to change people's lives. Going up in the lift at Covent Garden tube station, you will see men and women with that unmistakeable shining absent look in their eyes; the look of those obsessed and transfigured by thoughts of the loved one they are about to meet. They are exalted by the prospect of entering the presence of Verdi, of Aïda and Rhadames, of Placido Domingo and Monserrat Caballé, and have left their everyday selves far behind. Performers may be even more deeply involved. When they are under the spell, they will go to any trouble and make any sacrifice to achieve a perfect performance of a loved masterpiece. Like members of potlatch communities, who will heap together and destroy their most precious possessions to prove the strength of their faithfulness and the stretch of their hospitality, they will mortgage their houses, sell their cars, tape-recorders, or their wives' fur coats to pay for extra rehearsals or for the essential double-bass clarinet or wind-machine.

Veneration spreads from the masterworks and the men who created them to include all that pertains to them. Beethoven's eyeglasses, his second-best ear trumpet, his minor works, may be nothing much in themselves; it is memories of the Fifth Symphony that sanctifies them for us. We listen to a whole host of minor eighteenth-century symphonists and delight in their musical small talk because the style and idiom is close to that of Haydn and Mozart, and is irradiated by memories of those masters.

From the twentieth-century viewpoint, a masterpiece is a work which is as good as it could possibly be, and of which not a note could be changed without defacing its perfection. Such a view goes far to justifying the most extreme views on 'work-fidelity' commonly held today. Scholars spend years of their lives demonstrating the inevitability of masterpieces; something which few serious musicians like to question. Yet from a rational point of view, it is foolish to think that, because we cannot invent a better continuation for a Mozart exposition, Mozart himself might not have thought of a dozen. How far do we allow for the fact that any regularly repeated sequence of sounds or ideas acquires for us a sort of psychological inevitability; whether it is the alphabet or the Lord's Prayer? (When the BBC lengthened the last pip of the radio time-signal, angry listeners wrote in complaining of unwarranted interference with the true and proper order of things.) Wilfred Mellers once asked rhetorically: 'Why is it the great works of Haydn, Mozart, Beethoven, form indivisible wholes?' But if the movements of a dozen unfamiliar Haydn symphonies were shuffled into new combinations and appropriate transposed, how many of us would be able to sort them back into their original order?

Both the sense of inevitability and the work's power stem from sources within and without the work. 'The musical work of art', wrote Busoni, 'exists whole and intact before it has sounded and after the sound has finished'; expressing succinctly the faith of one for whom the essence of music lay in the ideal sounds shadowed forth in the score and only dimly realised in real-life performances. But from another point of view, the masterpiece is not a deathless work, but one that dies repeatedly and is capable of an infinite number of resurrections. It is less like a monument, the magnificent and grandiose conception of a single mind, than an oak tree, standing in a rich subsoil of past associations, present reactions, continually changing its outward form as the seasons change, and as winds and weather change. It is the product of collaboration between a master-composer with master-performers and, one hopes, master-listeners.

In the electronic age, we are exposed to music as never before. And so, the great works of the past become yet greater for us. As they accumulate associations to themselves, so the newly made works of later times, whatever their intrinsic qualities, are recognised by listeners as 'not in the same class'— for we have built up round them no knowledge of the hundred possible interpretations or the hundred strategies for listening that have gradually accumulated to the great music of known masters.

The cult of the masterpiece and the plight of the contemporary composer are closely bound up together. Inevitably, composers resent the apparently imperishable masterpieces which monopolise concert-hall time, hogging for themselves the sustaining attention of audiences. They are as dislikeable as the dreary megatheria of H. G. Wells's Rampole Island, which survived because they were there, living on the buds and growing shoots that might otherwise have proliferated to feed a multitude of other more brightly active species. Electronic technology and commercialised art between them have put pressure on the composer, forcing him to advance continually into new stylistic territory. He is driven from behind, by the living presence of the masters of the past. He is driven from below, by the host of commercial composers who exploit and devalue every expressive and technical device and spread their cheap imitations round the world. When I am in a pessimistic mood, I begin to think that, as the masterpieces of the past strengthen their hold on our minds and souls, the prospects for the masterpieces of the future grow steadily dimmer.

Nor can it any longer be taken as indisputable truth that the 'future of music' depends on the innovators who bring about change from high levels within the system. This is a creed to which we all pay lip-service; even the performers who devote their lives to the interpretation of classical music, the listeners who never go to contemporary-music concerts, the critics who would never miss a Schwarzkopf recital for a Stockhausen improvisation event, the conductors and promoters who resolutely avoid having anything to do with any music more daring than Bartók's, Stravinsky's Britten's, Shostakovich's.

Nor does the present enthusiasm of audiences and performers for the music of the past suggest that we would all grow pale and old, like the Gods in Valhalla, if all living composers were snatched away, Freia-like, tomorrow. Are there many who think that a lifetime spent with the music of Mozart, Beethoven, Berlioz or Stravinsky is a lifetime wasted? Of course we would be still better off if we enjoyed contemporary music as enthusiastically. But the belief that the 'future of music' depends on this or that development of language, form or idiom appears, from a realistic viewpoint, as implausible as the old Peruvian belief that man's soul would never reach a higher world except by crossing a bridge made of human hair; a feat to be accomplished only with the help of black dogs.

# VI

## QUESTIONS OF COMMUNICATION

THE MAN WITH much on his mind waits his turn in the queue at the phone box brooding on the message he hopes to transmit to a stranger of unknown intelligence. At last his turn comes; after many frustrations in the form of 'engaged' and 'line out of order' tones he gets through and presses his one and only 2p piece into the slot. He is connected! There is interference on the line; furiously he shakes the receiver, and the crackles become louder. The notice over the phone warns: *Speak slowly and clearly*, but he does not heed the warning. His mind is on the message rather than the stranger at the end of the line; to him the essential thing is that the message shall be transmitted in the pre-ordained form. At the end of two minutes, the pips sound, and he puts the receiver back on the holder, exhausted but content, and gives way to the next impatient caller. The message has been delivered.

It is not that he is trying deliberately to confuse or mystify, though this is how it may appear to the listener who complains 'why is modern music so difficult?'. Nor is he playing at message-sending; to him the message is really urgent, and he would angrily reject the suggestion that the carefully thought-out form of transmission may be inappropriate to the communication situation. Of course the fault is not his alone. Even willing and cooperative performers may be responsible for technical faults and crackles on the line. Listeners may perform prodigies of misunderstanding. But can anyone deny that a serious communication problem exists and that the composer bears some of the responsibility for it? At this stage (and at the risk of repeating some points that have been stressed already) we may be in a fair position to trace the faults in the line back to their causes.

The composer speaks the private language understood by his 'real' audience (fellow-composers, critics, members of reading panels, publishers), because it is they who respond, and so guide him, rather than the remote, hypothetical listener on the far end of the line. Today's composers inherit the uncompromising attitudes of the last great romantic individualists: Busoni, Schoenberg, Varèse. They recognise a sacred duty to transmit the message *in its one true form*; adopting Schoenberg's credo: 'It is my historic duty to write what destiny orders me to write.'

*Difficult* contemporary music is often produced as speeded-up car chases in old-comedy films were produced; by under-cranking. That is to say, it is composed in very slow motion, run through at top speed. Composers will lavish attention on every detail of a vast and complex score, and will pack in so much information that the communication channel is seriously overloaded (here too the example of Schoenberg, father-figure of so many serious composers, is influential). Such overloading may bring rewards after a work's fiftieth or hundredth performance; but when performances are so rare that possibilities of second, third or fourth hearings are remote, the density of closely micro-structured music, shorn of all repetitions, is daunting and confusing.

Under-cranking is often due to over-anxiety. Opportunities to address the public come so rarely, and are so important when they do come, that the composer feels bound to concentrate the message, packing in all he has to say regardless of the difficulties he is causing for listeners. In the same way, the castaway who is at last rescued from his desert island will pour out the contents of his mind in confused torrents of sound. It is hard for him to realise that, though he has an urgent need for self-expression, the listener may have a less urgent need to receive the message.

The age seems to 'select' composers of high intellect and convoluted modes of thought; and perhaps a convoluted puzzle-music is appropriate to the time we live in. It is also worth remembering that every culture has had its mysteries too sacred to be exposed in broad daylight. From the time of the Icelandic *skalds*, in which too much clarity was considered a technical fault, up to and beyond the days of Cockney rhyming slang, puzzles have been used to tease and stimulate, and often to extend and illuminate plain statements or to express the ineffable thoughts that cannot be expressed in everyday language. But there is a limit to the amount of teasing an unknown listener will take. Composers who venture out of their known milieu run the risk that the listener will become tired and confused, and will give up before he has discovered the answer to the riddle.

The bewildering rate at which styles and idioms are evolved and discarded is accelerated by technical advances and rising standards of performers. In the inter-war years (according to Ernst Roth and Theodor Adorno) the performer was often an unwilling collaborator, and contemporary music attracted second-rank specialists rather than virtuosi. But today, the dog dashes on ahead of his master; the performers set the pace, and composers strain to keep up; for in advanced music, the challenge to move up to—and just beyond—the limits of the possible can never be refused. The remoteness of the listener has increased the intimacy of the composer-performer relationship; avant-garde composers know better than their predecessors what will stimulate and delight performers. But in the games that develop between them, the listener may find that he is an unnoticed third party.

Naturally, the listener must take his share of responsibility for the communication failure. The great majority of knowledgeable music-lovers have little will to come to terms with contemporary music, and can give plausible excuses for staying away from every sort of modern-music concert. Intellectual music is 'too difficult' and 'too abstruse' and makes them feel excluded from the game. The music is written ostensibly for their benefit; but they stay on the side-lines like children watching their fathers playing with the trains off the Christmas tree. Middle-of-the-road contemporary music is 'too safe'; why listen to Robert Simpson when you might be listening to Sibelius or Nielsen, to Walton instead of Elgar, or Copland instead of Stravinsky? (These questions are, of course, only veiled excuses; there are plenty of good reasons for listening to all three.) Avant-garde music 'plays for effect'; makes absurd noises and uses instruments in ways which affront their natures; is 'pretentious' or 'in doubtful taste'. And so, the listener frees himself of his obligations to contemporary music.

It is tragic that contemporary music still wears such a fearful face for so many intelligent listeners; particularly when so much excellent music has been brought into the world in the last fifty years which would, given sympathetic performance and understanding audiences, enrich many lives. We may have no great composers today; but we have numbers of resourceful and inventive craftsmen, many minor poets and some sound-engineers of formidable powers. It is an absurd position that, with so much talk of order and logic, unity and inevitability, in music, we cannot bring order and logic into our own musical interrelationships or promote the most important unity of all—that binding link between composer and listener, without which the act of composition becomes mere self-indulgence. But the gap grows no smaller. Audiences have not yet come to terms with Schoenberg's music, which is as simple compared to Elliott Carter's as Mozart's is compared to Schoenberg's. To suppose that *one day* audiences will come to appreciate Carter, Boulez or Babbitt as if by magic is as absurd as to suppose that a widening trade gap will suddenly vanish if we look the other way.

*Power of the word*
It is not only contemporary music that poses us with communication problems. For all music is by nature mysterious, elusive and untranslatable, its fascination and power lying in its ambiguity, its ability to say many things to many people. This does not discourage us from trying to elucidate its meaning, sometimes in symbols or graphs, but most often in words. For Western man's first instinct when confronted with a problem is to talk it over. Words are still the most powerful tools at his disposal, and he preserves a naïve belief that with their help every problem can, in time, be forced to yield up a solution. A few musicians may maintain, with Mendelssohn, that 'music is more definite than speech, and to want to explain it by means of words is to make the meaning obscure'. But even among the most complete musicians there are few who never feel the urge to pin down, in words, whatever it is that music seems to be saying, or to amplify musical experience by their commentaries.

Marshall McLuhan believes that the printed word is on the way out and that the visual (and especially the televisual) image will soon take over the word's functions. Jacques Barzun suggests that the growing popularity of music is a symptom of our increasing resistance to words, and of a deep-lying demand 'not so much for silence as for the wordless sign'. Yet in the 1970s, the passion for music is linked with a passion for verbal commentaries: interviews with performers and composers; articles on backstage musical life; analytical and polemical essays on music itself, considered from every likely and unlikely angle.

While the publication of printed music declines, the publication of words-about-music increases year after year. No specialist group is without its news-sheet or magazine. The shelves of the libraries expand to take in ever more histories, books on the theory and practice of music of all ages, full-length biographies of composers whose works are seldom if ever heard in the concert hall.

→ The remarkable increase in the number of books on music published in the post-war years is a sign that music (as a subject to be written about) has passed the economic watershed and become good business. There are now, in the English-speaking world, enough music-lovers, and often enough specialists in a particular field, to justify publication of every sort of book, from scholarly studies of medieval church composers to popular, journalistic public-and-private lives of great conductors and opera stars. But the expansion of the word-industry is not only due to the favourable market conditions. It is a symptom of our need to provide ourselves with handles for understanding; doubly necessary when we receive sounds disembodied and out of context through radio and recording. It also reflects a general tendency to take experience at second hand. We view the world through the television screen; we scan the fashion and cookery pages of the Sunday supplements with no thought of buying the clothes or trying out the recipes; or, at one remove further, we read reviews of travel books with no intention of reading the books, and even less intention to follow in the travellers' footsteps.

So too in music. We show greater enthusiasm for workshop programmes, critics' discussions of contemporary works, or interviews with composers, than for music itself. This new balance of interests is reflected in market prices. In later life, Stravinsky could earn more from a ten-minute television interview than from a new symphony. Cage's books and lectures have earned him a comfortable income while his music remains largely unperformed.

One result of the public's increased appetite for words-about-music has been the emergence of a new generation of eloquent, entertaining composers, as skilled in the arts of being interviewed as they are in their own craft. Stockhausen, Berio and Kagel are all word-and-music men; their ideas are often expressed so persuasively and convincingly in words that we find it hard to tell whether the explanations or the music which follows give us most satisfaction.

Even in a more or less free society, we are all of us afraid of the power of the word. Of the eloquent orator, who can persuade us to take action against our better judgement; of the dogged propagandist who wears us down by persistently repeating the same message; of the smearer (at high political or gossip-column level) whose insinuations leave traces of doubt and suspicion in our minds, even though we angrily reject them; of the copywriters and reviewers who, as Cyril Ray once remarked, are so skilled that 'they can probably put into wines and foods tastes and other attributes that are not really there at all'.

And if into foods, why not into music? Critics, analysts, and composers themselves can direct our attention, colour our reactions to music all the more easily because music itself speaks cryptically and indirectly, appealing to us at deeper levels where words have no currency. The attitudes of a whole generation may be formed and set by the words they have read about music; Busoni and Schoenberg have influenced us as much through their writings as through their compositions. Hanslick, Newman and Tovey defined a repertory and established a scale of musical values for their readers and disciples. The word-men may be only parasites on the musical body, though it would be kinder and perhaps more realistic to describe them as symbiotes. Whether parasites or symbiotes, they have a considerable effect on the health and behaviour of their host, and for that reason we have to take them seriously.

Much power is often ascribed to music critics; but the influence they exercise is, and should be, short-term. They are correspondents, sending in hasty reports from the battle-front, and cannot be expected to give a detached or over-all view of the action. In England, the critic is generally saved from having to take too much responsibility on to his own shoulders, for he is generally only one of many similar observers, each reporting the scene from his own viewpoint and according to his own prejudices.

Nowhere in the world is there a music critic whose influence can be compared with that of Clive Barnes, formerly of the *New York Times*, who could decide the fate of plays and musicals, in which hundreds of thousands of dollars and thousands of hours of skilled work had been invested, with a single unfavourable notice. It is hard to imagine how theatre-goers could allow themselves to be swayed so easily; one can only assume that the balance between failure and success was as precarious as it often is on the stock exchange, where the slightest and most unreliable indicators of the state of the market may determine the fate of a new issue. But the music critic's role seems to be that of entertainer rather than adjudicator and prophet. Even a successful critic's fan mail is small compared with that of a woman's-page writer, and is largely concerned with names he has misspelt or which have been misprinted. Neville Cardus once noted that if he misquoted the batting average of a cricketer of the 1920s, he would be snowed under with letters; but that if he got a Beethoven opus number wrong, no one seemed to care.

Critics today have mostly dropped the pontifical, polemical tone that was popular in the inter-war years. This is partly because we are no longer so sure that there is any one true faith to be defended. It is also due to the fact that the general public is now so well educated, through record and radio, that we no longer think it appropriate to pose as teachers and masters. The range of concerts, from medieval to avant-garde, is so wide that the general-purpose critic will often find himself as much out of his depth as the rest of the audience. In these circumstances, he acts as a music-taster with no claims to superior knowledge; this is not a bad thing in so far as it reduces the gap between specialist and non-specialist and does not demote the listener to an inferior level. Today, as in the past, most critics steer clear of all controversial matters not directly concerned with music. The isolation of the musical state-within-a-state is nowhere so clearly shown as in English music criticism, where one of the leading left-wing weeklies, the *New Statesman*, devotes most of its music articles to criticisms of opera, most luxurious of all entertainments, written in a style and tone as high as that of any of the establishment right-wing papers.

Critics, like audiences, are today very rarely shocked or outraged by any sort of avant-garde music. They are far more inclined to give young composers the benefit of any doubt than their predecessors, and can generally be considered as 'friends of new music'. One reason for this new-found tolerance seems to be that, while Wagner, Strauss, or Schoenberg seemed to threaten the established order, it is clear today that no musical revolution is going to displace the established masterworks, and that Beethoven will not suffer if Britten and Berio are also allowed their place in the sun. Critics may be kind to new works because they know in their hearts that they are probably writing their obituaries. Hopefully, they suggest: 'This work should (or must) be heard again.' But they are voicing only a faint hope; pressure on performance space ensures that only a tiny proportion will achieve second or third performances.

Today, the fiercest wars are waged, not against rebels who threaten the stability of the musical state, but against contemporary composers who continue to work in outmoded idioms, reminding us of neo-classical Stravinsky, or Hindemith, or (worse still) of Sibelius or Vaughan Williams. It is curious and sad that, even when we admire such works and think them quite as interesting as the models they are founded on, we can still sense that they do not belong in the present scheme of things. Intellectually, we can tell ourselves that it matters not in the least that Bach was old-fashioned in his day, and that even Elgar's lack of progressive instincts now seems irrelevant; but we cannot get over the fact that Malcolm Arnold, Robert Simpson or Peter Wishart are continuing to write music that is not of the age. How far this feeling of the 'spirit of the age' is confined to critics and other hardened concert-goers, and how far it is shared by the general public, I would not like to say.

Critics also act as barometers of the age in being hot for authenticity, giving no quarter to those who cut or re-orchestrate or start trills on the wrong note. (Again, it would be risky to assume that the general public feels strongly about such matters.) Like performers and recording engineers, we are apt to regard technical perfection as an end in itself, and are genuinely shocked by minute lapses in ensemble or intonation that would have passed unnoticed twenty years ago. We comment on the presence or absence of the cymbal clash in Bruckner's Seventh Symphony (surely an unmomentous point if there ever was one) with as much gravity as motoring correspondents commenting on the position of a windscreen-wiper switch or the size of the ashtrays in the Mark IV model of a familiar car.

Critics address a small public, and do not serve as guides to future events, as do drama and film critics. What is it then that we have to offer? No doubt arts criticism still gives a certain *cachet* to quality papers, and no doubt (in England) the system rolls along under its own momentum because things have always been that way. But it could also be that criticism is needed more than ever today, because so many listen to music away from the throng and far from the sources of sound. It fills in a material and human background, provides a general context within which the listener's imagination can operate, reassuring him that there are others who care as much as he does for the loved art. And for those whose knowledge is rudimentary, there is the pleasure we can get from watching a strange game. We may not have the least idea what is going on; but we like to observe intelligent people engaged seriously and intently in the cut-and-thrust of their own affairs.

Theorists and analytical writers of every age come to terms with music in their own ways, one age's understanding often becoming the next age's misunderstanding. No one now remembers Day's elaborate theories which explained complex harmonies as being derived from multiple roots. Riemann's laborious analyses-by-phrasing, recorded in complete editions of the classics, are of no interest to today's theorists. We respect Schenker for his conception of the *ur-linie* and of whole movements as immensely elaborated, backward-stretching cadences. But both Schenker and Reti (who tried to explain the apparent unity of great works by relating all developments to basic master-motives) are already figures of the past, their theories bypassed by those who favour semi-mathematical forms of statistical and linguistic analysis.

The fact that many interpretations and analyses seem to be mutually exclusive should not worry us too much. They can't all be right, but maybe all have caught a glimpse of some central rightness. Schweitzer sees biblical symbolism in every rising fifth or drooping scale in a Bach choral prelude; Reti, attacked by acute monothemania, derives the whole of Bach's B minor Mass from a single four-note motive. Tovey accounts for the almost endless sequence of final chords that concludes Beethoven's Fifth Symphony on the principle of golden sections; Xenakis analyses a Beethoven sonata in terms of vectors, by a process no one but he himself can follow. Such views would have made Bach's or Beethoven's eyes pop out of their heads with wonder. But the twentieth century needs to rediscover music on its own terms; and the spiritual children of Freud and Schoenberg are bound to the view that what appears on the surface is only the manifestation of forces acting at deep, unconscious levels. When Mellers says, of the famous opening chords of *Tristan*: 'their harmonically interlocking perfect and imperfect fourths are a consummate musical symbol for the simultaneous joy and anguish of the sexual act', we should not pedantically object that no one can hear the interlocking fourths in a four-note chord, but accept the poetic image. Much flowery descriptive writing is really poetic fantasy, and we should no more object to it than we should object to the poet who describes his mistress as a fair gazelle. If he insisted that she really was a fair gazelle that would be different; and it is when writers like Riemann or Reti exalt their personal fantasies into factual accounts of 'what really happens' that we should beware of taking them as seriously as they take themselves.

The severer analytical methods of our own time, which mainly emanate from American universities, can only be understood by the very few—scholars, students and composers—who operate on the same closed circuit. For today, as in the past, scholar-musicians form a distinct species, with their own style of musicality, and are often only remotely interested in the world where music is performed in the presence of large, unlearned audiences. Universities tend to attract those whose thought-processes are ingenious and subtle; as plainer issues are settled, research workers move on into ever more remote and specialised areas, and the nature of the work in turn draws in those who are fitted for it. Particularly in fields of theory and analysis, the work takes on a momentum of its own, and all connection with practical musical matters is lost. Conversely, there are very few performers who would dream of consulting the *Journal of Music Theory* before tackling a Beethoven sonata. The position is very much like the one-time position in ancient China, where the wise men spent their time defining the scales and modes which, for the good of the state and to ensure next year's harvest, were to be officially recognised, while practical musicians went on their way, evolving their own scales, in ignorance of all theoretical systems.

There is one area in which the writing of words-about-music seems to raise almost insoluble problems. When difficult new music is played in public, it is only common sense that someone should explain to the audience in advance, in speech or more usually in the programme notes, what they may be in for. For the rules of the musical game are constantly changing, and we will no more make sense of George Crumb's *Black Angels* if we listen to it with expectations tuned as for Britten's Second Quartet, than we would make sense of golf if we expected the game to be played to a time-limit. Yet note-writers, and most of all composers, seem to be under a compulsion to describe in detail constructive processes which will never be apparent in sound. Sometimes they seem to be apologising for the difficulty of the music; to be saying, in effect: 'The sounds may mean little to you; but let me tell you how systematically and with how much art they are put together.' I have been at concerts where specialists and critics as well as the public were unable to correlate the sounds with the programme notes, and where tentative applause at the end showed that no one was at all sure whether we had reached the end of the work. For lay audiences, struggling in a sea of strange sounds with the programme note as their only lifeline, the effect can be bewildering and depressing. Too often, the notes confirm the impression that contemporary music is hard work and that the listener who misses the retrograde inversion at the third bar after G has somehow failed the exam. He is reduced to the status of second-class citizen; hanger-on at a cultural event above his level.

We may take the view that writing about music is necessarily *difficult* when music itself is *difficult;* and that to write down to the level of one's audience in words is as great a sin as to write down in music. But it is not so much a question of writing down as of writing appropriately; and this is where too many well-meaning mediators strike blank. They seem to have only the vaguest ideas of the ways in which real audiences respond, and to consider that if they have described the technical processes involved in a work's composition, they have fulfilled their function. The failure of commentators to assess an audience's needs and limitations is only part of a larger malaise. Often, composers themselves are equally at a loss. Unable to form any clear conception of the hypothetical listener, they dismiss him from their minds. I have heard Boulez say that his job is to compose and present music; he leaves it to others to find out what, if anything, audiences will make of it. Babbitt, in a famous essay, 'Who Cares if You Listen?', went further:

> Why should the layman be other than bored or puzzled by music he cannot understand? ... The time has passed when the normally well-educated man without special preparation could understand the most advanced work in, for example, mathematics, philosophy, and physics. Advanced music, to the extent that it reflects the knowledge and originality of the informed composer, scarcely can be expected to appear

more intelligible than these arts and sciences to the person whose musical education has been even less extensive than his background in other fields.

Boulez and Babbitt seem to be saying, with the poet Grillparzer: 'I strove for effect on no one but myself.' It may be a noble maxim, but in an age when men speak with a babel of tongues, it is a dangerous one to follow rigorously.

*End of the line*
In discussing problems of communication, we have been over and over again drawn back to consider the sender of the message. For he is the active one, the wooer who seeks to be understood and accepted. We complain that he behaves in difficult and enigmatic ways; but there is enigma too in the silence at the other end of the line. The listener is the passive, veiled beauty who will not lift even a corner of her veil until the wooer has declared himself; the composer sings his songs not even sure whether Susanna or the Countess is hidden behind it. Yet the one at the end of the line is in some ways the most interesting and important of the three protagonists: composer, performer, and listener. He or she represents the unknown factor in the musical equation, which will never be solved if its value cannot be determined. We need to know how people listen or fail to listen even more than we need to know how we would like them to listen. However unsatisfactory and fragmentary the evidence—and however unreliable as a witness the listener proves to be—we cannot dismiss it as irrelevant or of no interest. Which is why, having almost reached the end of this book, I want to direct attention to the one at the end of the line.

'The public ear', said Samuel Butler, 'is like a common. There is not much to be got off it, but that little is for the most part grazed by geese and donkeys.' The audience can communicate its intensest reactions to music no more articulately than geese or donkeys, and generally it is those who bray and cackle loudest who make their presence felt most keenly. Opera audiences will cheer, boo, shout advice to singers and conductors, and from their applause we can deduce a crude scale of values. The loudest, highest cadential notes win the most vociferous applause from simpler-minded opera fans; the connoisseurs wait to see how certain notoriously taxing passages are brought off, and hasten to get in their *bravissimas* so that their discrimination can be properly appreciated.

Concert audiences are less communicative. They listen quietly to the music, and clap in conventional ways in the proper places. You cannot tell whether they are applauding music, performers, from a sense of relief that the piece is over, or out of kind-heartedness because everyone seems to have tried hard. People occasionally walk out during modern works which offend them; but those who remain rarely fail to clap. Like the statue of the Commendatore, they can make only one response —the gesture of acceptance. The very worst a composer or performer can expect is frosty silence; which, as Roberto Gerhard once remarked, 'deprives one even of the relief of being angry'.

The good behaviour of concert audiences—who no longer even clap between concerto movements (not even at the end of the first movement of Tchaikovsky's Violin Concerto, where the layout of the last few pages seems designed to elicit frenzied applause as a coda to what has gone before)—is not necessarily a sign of good musical health. Audiences can be too passive, too willing to be worked on rather than to participate in the work, too apt (in England) to behave as though they were in church. Not to smile at Haydn's best jokes, or even to recognise the possibility that serious composers are only 'serious' in so far as they are concentrated on and fully committed to their job. Audiences today are infinitely tolerant, but not necessarily therefore broad-minded. They will put up with anything without protest, but in a spirit of endurance, and out of a sense of duty.

The politeness, inertia and unshockability of today's audiences is no doubt partly due to the conditioning effects of radio and recording. There is no point in clapping our favourite violinist or booing the latest avant-garde work when we hear it over the air or on record, so we get out of the habit of participating in the performance, whether recorded or live. Perhaps the rackety conditions of modern life also incline us to take things easy in the concert hall. But it is curious that audiences at pop concerts still behave very much as audiences at nineteenth-century piano recitals behaved; noisily demanding their favourite pieces, like the Parisians who refused to listen to Liszt's Beethoven until he had played the Fantasia from *Robert le Diable*.

We are shocked that so great a musician as Liszt should have needed to submit to the orders of vulgar, illiterate audiences, and are even inclined to blame him for not taking a firmer stand against them. But Liszt was a child of his time; living in the tail-end of a period when artists generally accepted the proposition 'the audience (or the patron) is always right' even while rebelling against it. Reaction followed; Schoenberg and Stravinsky took up the polemic position 'the audience is always wrong' (though Stravinsky at any rate, and fortunately for us, rarely lived up to his intransigent public attitudes). At least 'the audience is always wrong' implies some sort of relationship with an audience. Today, composers, and to a lesser degree performers, get the feeling 'the audience is not really there at all'. The quality of silence—in the broadcasting studio and in the concert hall—often has a profoundly disturbing effect. Performers play for themselves or for each other; the avant-garde composer, suspecting that his latest horror is only a Dracula with rubber teeth—since it fails to draw blood—is driven on to further extravagances.

It is doubly important today that we should learn to read through the audience's silences. In the electronic age, performers and composers are increasingly isolated from the main part of their audience, so that the reactions of the live audiences are significant not only for their own sakes, but as a sample of the reactions of the larger, inaccessible audiences of radio and recording. There are, however, various methods, none very satisfactory, by which we can investigate audiences' responses: by direct questioning; by observation and inference; and by the crude but still informative method of studying box office returns.

Stupid questions get stupid answers; but the results of questionnaires suggest that there are no sensible questions that can be put to listeners. If they are asked to describe their reactions to music, a fine froth of random wordage rises to the surface. Most are without words to describe their deeper experiences, and seem to skim off the vague and fleeting thoughts that pass through their minds while they listen. Those questioned by Vernon Lee in her book *Music and its Lovers* (published in 1932 but still as far as I know the only serious and protracted study of emotional responses to have been carried out by a competent and perceptive investigator) seem at first to transmit no information about music though much about themselves. Only an upper-class English gentlewoman would interpret the *Egmont* Overture in terms of a persecuted horse, 'its dying eyes looking with patience into the fiery ball of the sun'; or would have the confidence to utter aloud some of their stranger verbal fantasies. One hears 'jolly bears dancing' in the Archduke Trio. Another, in an attempt at more specific definition, says: 'with Mozart the tunes are apt to come out stringy'. Wagner's music 'makes you feel like after a debauch'.

Contemporary investigations carried out in an up-to-date statistical spirit are hardly more illuminating; or else tell us only about the negative aspects of listening. It is easy enough to establish what we already know—that listeners are swayed by extraneous factors. Bach is less acceptable if listeners are told that Buxtehude is the composer; the same radio series attracts more listeners when the title is changed from 'classical' to 'popular'. Who wants to know that untrained listeners prefer wide vibrato, or that the 'enjoyment ratings' of an unspecified audience in an unspecified place were 34·7 for Stravinsky's *Soldier's Tale* and 71·1 for Beethoven's Fifth Symphony?

It is no doubt partly because direct questioning elicits such an incoherent response from lay listeners that highly educated and literate musicians form the lowest opinions of listeners' mentality and have no desire to probe further into the nature of that mentality. Ernest Newman once wrote: 'I am quite willing to learn something new about Beethoven, but I have no time to waste in reading how Beethoven affects Tom, Dick, or Harry.' Virgil Thomson writes scornfully of 'ladies who have been going to concerts since childhood and still only recognize 8 pieces out of the 50 in the repertoire ... what they like is (1) the conductor (2) the resemblance of the music executor's superfinish to that of other streamlined luxury products with which our lives are surrounded. They feel at home among "nice" things.' Composers tend to rate the intellectual perception of music higher than the emotional, and suspect audiences of having no musical-intellectual capacity at all. Thus, Stravinsky writes: 'What disturbs me about [*Wozzeck*] ... is the level of its appeal to "ignorant" audiences, with which one may attribute its success to: (1) the story; (2) Bible, child sentiment; (3) sex; (4) brevity; (5) dynamics, pppp to ffff; (6) muted brass, ⟩, ▼, *col legno*, etc.; (7) the idea that it is being modern.'

The type of listening most highly valued by educated

musicians—and perhaps the only kind that can be rationally discussed—could be labelled 'constructive listening'. Hindemith named the intellectual listening process *co-construction*, and describes it clearly in *A Composer's World*. His hypothetical auditor

> while listening to the musical structure, as it unfolds before his ears, is mentally constructing parallel to it and simultaneously with it a mirrored image. Registering the composition's components as they reach him he tries to match them with their corresponding parts of his mental construction. Or he merely surmises the composition's presumable course, and compares it with the image of a musical structure which he has stored away in his memory....

This is the sort of educated listening which is generally recognised as *superior*, even by those who can never hope to share it. One of Vernon Lee's subjects wrote with awe of this promised land she would never enter: 'you must distinguish from music the effects of rhythm like e.g. a drum and the timbre of instruments... which can give you the human physical emotion. But that is not music. MUSIC is written on paper... it is the intervals etc. And these are intellectual not sensorial things.'

Constructive listening is only possible for those with reasonably well-developed memories and powers of discrimination; but there is no doubt at all that these can be developed in a fairly high proportion of listeners. Tests conducted by Seashore and later musical psychologists confirm the potential ability of many of us to remember tunes, identify timbres, harmonies and rhythms, and themes in straightforward transformations. We are, in fact, educable in the sense that we could learn to listen to music in the Hindemithian manner: following through the action in anticipation, teased or gratified as expectations are confounded or confirmed, shadow-composing a familiar work as it proceeds.

Yet anyone who has taught children or music students can confirm that only a small minority have a natural spontaneous interest in formal processes and long-term relationships; and that many, not necessarily from lack of capacity, show not the least interest in changing their listening habits. And that among those who (for psychological or physiological reasons) have the greatest difficulty in hearing an inside part or identifying a recondite harmony there are a great many who are aware and sensitive musicians, keenly responsive to the tone of voice and what we could vaguely describe as the 'message' of the music, and able to appraise the quality of an interpretation with some assurance.

It is often suggested by intellectual musicians that this sort of instinctive listener is somehow appreciating the constructional and architectural qualities of a Beethoven symphony or a Bartók concerto at subliminal level; and I can believe that experts trained in analytical listening may have an intuition of logical processes even when they can't identify them. I know myself the feeling of believing that there is a canon or retrograde inversion hidden in the maze of counterpoint in a complex Schoenberg piece. What I find unbelievable, is that the listener who has never consciously followed through developments or transformations will have even a rudimentary or subconscious understanding of the elaborate and often abstruse compositional processes of Berg, Boulez or Elliott Carter.

But there is no need to assume that listeners of this sort are therefore musical morons, or snobs who attend concerts merely to follow the fashion. The conclusion we should draw is that there are many more routes to enjoyment and to understanding (different sorts of understanding) than are allowed for by the musical map-makers and guides. Instinctive listeners of perception and sensibility who are constantly exposed to music (as so many are today) develop their own modes of understanding; like the shepherd who spends his life in one mountainous lakeland area, who will read many signs he does not identify in words; knows the size and steepness of each hill through the hunger in his stomach or the aching of his legs; registers a thousand phenomena of the moment (passing clouds; the strength of wind in the bracken's bending; the coming storm in the feel of the air on his skin) rather as the instinctive listener registers the tone and atmosphere of a particular performance. If you ask him to show you the way on your map, he will often be at a loss, and may have the vaguest idea as to distances in miles between towns or villages, and even less about the geological strata of his homeland. And if they are taxed with their lack of knowledge, shepherds (and likewise naïve but experienced listeners) might answer, as the father of the Indian prince Modupe answered: 'The things that hurt one do not show on a map. The truth of a place is the joy and hurt that comes from it.'

I would also suggest (basing the suggestion partly on personal experience) that even those who are fairly skilled map-readers do not habitually follow through music in any orderly rational way. In a live performance, there are many attractions and counter-attractions; some directly connected with the music, some frivolous. According to William James, 'There is no such thing as voluntary attention sustained for more than a few seconds at a time. What is called sustained voluntary attention is a repetition of successive efforts which bring back the topic to the mind.' We skirt around the musical topic; sometimes following thematic progress, sometimes responding to a particularly apt or inept piece of phrasing or articulation (and comparing it in our minds with past interpretations); sometimes simply succumbing to the power of sound—though in a familiar work, an unexpected cut or a fudged bassoon entry may suddenly awaken our inward monitor which is keeping up with events even while we are dreaming.

And I see no reason why many instinctive but experienced listeners should not attend to the music in very much this way. We can imagine listeners of every grade and species from those for whom music is like a superior sort of chess game, to those who submit willingly as music arouses in them a series of unnameable emotions. Certainly intellectual listeners get emotional satisfaction out of their musical chess games; and it seems equally probable that instinctive listeners do appreciate order, symmetry, the complex patterning of Bach's counterpoint, on their own untranslatable terms. As Vernon Lee, who was herself a musical innocent, poetically remarks: 'The multitudinousness of Bach's uninterrupted outpourings forces some of us to much the same reverential acquiescence as the sight of the inscrutable starry heavens.' The spirit behind these words is Apollonian, and implies an appreciation of the rightness of order, of everything being in its proper place.

I also see no reason why Virgil Thomson's concert-goers should not at the same time like 'nice things nicely done' and gain, through repeated exposure, some knowledge of what the great composers were after. In a broad sense, most popular composers still take the audience with them. I cannot believe that most concert-hall listeners don't feel the tension and expectation in the air during the long dominant pedal leading to the Finale of Beethoven's Fifth Symphony, and feel joyous relief when it resolves in a blazing C major; or that they haven't at some time been disconcerted by the false starts of the trio in the same symphony; or that most listeners haven't, simply by exposure, come to feel the different effects of conventional cadences, and would not rise in outrage if a classical symphony ended with an interrupted cadence and the supertonic chord. The fact that most listeners feel 'at sea' in difficult modern music and 'at home' in classical music suggests at least that they recognise home when they come to it, in the form of a perfect cadence. One reason they don't understand Schoenberg is because they understand Beethoven too well, and can't get rid of their ideas about what music should be like. Yet the encouraging thing about our age, is that listening habits are changing, and are more fluid than at any previous time in history.

There must be a higher proportion of *experienced* listeners among today's audiences than at any time in the last 200 years. Though it is sometimes suggested that there has been a decline in the number of active amateurs since the days when every middle-class home contained a piano, there are far more today who have reached a high level of skill and knowledge over a far wider range.* Still more numerous and significant is the audience of record and radio users, who expose themselves to the sounds of music of all styles and periods in massive doses, till the sounds of their favourite works are imprinted on their minds. As I suggested earlier, this new generation of listeners has become sensitised to the finest nuances of timbre and is often expert in assessing and comparing performances of familiar works. At the same time, they are more given to casual and non-consecutive listening, so that they are even less likely than the listeners of the past to be keenly aware of overall forms and long-term relationships.

'Il ne suffit pas que l'artiste soit préparé pour le public, il faut aussi que le public le soit à ce qu'on va lui faire entendre', wrote Baillot. But this is the age of the unprepared listener. Music enters into our everyday lives from the time the alarm

* At a master class given in 1977 by the Cleveland Quartet in the South Bank Summer Festival (which draws in a largely non-specialist audience) all but three of an audience of about 200 declared themselves able to read music.

clock goes off in the morning; I know people who are sung or played to sleep by their bedside radio. It is the age of the distracted listener (I borrow the phrase from Walter Benjamin) when we appropriate music to ourselves as we appropriate the buildings we live in. We don't appreciate the architectural qualities of our homes as a visiting group of architectural students would appreciate them; and it is likely that the visitors will be distressed at some of the uses we make of these monuments to architects' glory, running up lean-to sheds that destroy their symmetry, putting in partition walls in the lovingly designed open-plan living room *cum* kitchen *cum* playroom. Architects are aggrieved at the way their visions of ideal living are ignored and overridden. As John Ludovici once said: 'Because privacy involves barriers it plays hell with your elevations.' But at least the houses they build are used; and in a way (if not in the architect's way) appreciated. And so too music is used, even if traditionalists are horrified by the casual and disrespectful ways in which it is handled.

And it seems to me possible that the future lies with these new distracted listeners, rather than with the tiny groups of specialists at new-music concerts; and that composers may revert to the attitudes of 200 years ago, no longer expecting to form and educate listeners, waking up to the truth that there exists a potential public of wide if shallow experience, high sensibility, and considerable powers of discrimination. How this will ever happen, I have not an idea; but if composers could tune in again to their listeners—as Haydn and even Beethoven tuned in to theirs—the prospects for the future would be brighter.

# VII

## SPIRIT OF THE AGE

IN AN OMNIVOROUS, polycultural age, when reputations go up and down like shuttlecocks and every commentator constructs a different family tree of influential composers, there are all too many 'spirits of the age' about, interacting or pointedly avoiding each other's company. Who can say why Rachmaninov and Elgar, cold-shouldered by the élite for so long, are now back in favour? Why Vivaldi out-sells Haydn in the record shops, or why so many much-admired composers of the '40s and '50s have altogether vanished from view? To a great extent, these many 'spirits' are not the spirit of the age in any cosmic sense, but represent the collective opinions of the informed and articulate: critics, historians, dictionary-makers, composers, conductors and performers who happen to possess strong views and the gift of words. Most music-lovers never realised or admitted that Elgar and Sibelius were *out*, and knew too little of the politics of contemporary music to align themselves with Boulez, Stockhausen, Cardew or Morton Feldman. If you suggested that Schoenberg had changed the face of music, they could reasonably point out that nothing much seemed to have changed at all.

But there have been great changes in the internal metabolism of the body musical: a reordering of the constitution of the musical state, which has affected all its members. It is in these changes rather than in changes of style and idiom that the changing 'spirit of the age' can best be identified—that, at any rate, has been the underlying theme of this book. The leading motives in this fugue of composers, performers, listeners and entrepreneurs can now be quickly summarised and assembled:

It is the age of expansion. The bees have moved into new hives, but still dance their old dances.

It is the age of the superior performer, whose skills and status have risen, till he has become the unacknowledged leader in areas where the composer once exercised supreme authority.

It is the age of the disorientated composer, whose audience

has been distanced and dispersed so that he has difficulty in identifying any target at all.

It is the age of the experienced but distracted listener, who has acquired by exposure an intimate knowledge of music and the power to distinguish many tones of voice without, necessarily, being able to follow what is being communicated.

It is the age of the most effective secret alliances the world has yet seen between music, commerce, and technology.

It is the age of reverence; of old works endlessly repeated, and of contemporary works endlessly neglected.

It is the age of separated extremes. When high art tolerates no compromise while low art says: 'everything can be arranged.' When high art can only focus on posterity, while low art cannot see beyond tomorrow. When high art ignores the common listener, while low art prostrates itself at his feet. It is the age of the totally controlled and the totally free;* of the smoothest perfection and the most deliberate roughness.†

It is the age (as every age has been) of the submerged middle-cultures; of those who go on as they have always gone on, without concerning themselves with the march of progress or the 'spirit of the age'.

In any age it would be possible to list extreme styles and extreme attitudes and so to give an impression of the bewildering variety and scope of the music of the age. The striking difference between our own culture and earlier cultures is, that these extremes represent the ends of a discontinuous, or almost discontinuous spectrum. Many commentators (including Leonard Meyer, Willi Reich and Eric Salzman) have pointed out that we seem to be moving into a polycultural society, where the mainstream of musical development has divided into many smaller streams and where no mainstream can be identified. Yet though *separation* of cultural streams is so clearly marked, the movements I have been describing have not been

---

* For instance: of Cornelius Cardew's *Treatise*: in which no instructions at all are given for the interpretation of freely drawn symbols, the order of pages in the score, the instruments to be used, or the effects to be aimed at.

† For instance: of the Portsmouth Sinfonia: a group of students, most of whom could not read music or play any instruments, who nevertheless put on orchestral concerts during the early 1970s, programmes including such 'popular classics' as the Overture to Rossini's *William Tell*.

independent or random movements. Art-music and commercial music—totally organised intellectual and wildest avant-garde\*—refined lieder-singers and football fans with their coarse and lusty songs—are still related even though separated and antipathetic to one another. There is a balance of opposing extremes; of reactions and anti-reactions. Compensating movements towards or away from the centre may be read as steps in a dance as complex as that of courting pigeons, in which movements of advance or (just as often) of retreat must be presumed to conform to underlying laws of behaviour, even if we, from our limited viewpoint, do not hold the clues that would elucidate them.

The present state of tension-between-extremes may be partly explainable along the following lines.

In the age of television, record and radio, the world beats its way into our consciousness whether we will or no. For the average passive listener, this presents no special problems. He allows music to flow round him and through him, and is borne along by the stream. But for serious and dedicated professionals, who want to be in control of their destinies, things are not so simple. The eighteenth-century court composer could spend a lifetime in the service of one patron, master in his own domain and able to ignore, if he so wished, not only world trends but the musical trends of neighbouring courts. If he grew eager for experience, he went out in search of it. But today, Boulez in Paris cannot fail to feel the anti-influence of Morton Feldman in America. Commerce forces on us its homogenised world-product. Influences which in a more leisurely age we might have absorbed into our systems become threats to our identity.† Our defence is to assert a still more fiercely personal or group identity. The élitists rush on ahead to find the still undiscovered beach unmarked by human footprints. Professional performers withdraw from the world arena to devote themselves to the more private sorts of medieval or avant-garde music. To save our souls, we insulate ourselves against change, withdraw and

\* Boulez aims 'to annihilate the self in favour of a predetermining system'. Morton Feldman declares that 'every note of my music is inspired; there is no pre-conceived system'.

† The sudden and bewildering variety of experience offered in a great university can act in music the same way on students straight from school. After teaching at Baltimore, Richard Rodney Bennett noted how such students 'are often numbed and driven back into themselves by the richness and diversity of contemporary musical experience'.

attempt to separate ourselves from the influences we cannot escape from, even if we never leave our homes.

The intellectual and literate world reacted rather differently when the invention of printing threw open the doors of the past, allowing all men access to the wisdom and poetry of all times and all places. Printing stimulated the world's appetite for knowledge and led to a great upsurge of new creative activity. Renaissance man, however, had more time to absorb and digest the effects of that revolution, and greater control over the use of the new communication medium. We have little time and little choice; and here lies the cause of many difficulties and uncertainties. How do we plot our new course in suddenly changed circumstances? Which opportunities should we accept and which reject? Who is for us and who is against us?

*Diabolos in Musica*

> Octava deficiens et superflua
> Sunt duo diaboli in Musica

wrote Heinichen, early in the eighteenth century, in his *Der Generalbass in der Composition*. But the best-known and longest-lived devil in music is the melodic tritone, an interval disallowed by Palestrina and by the church composers and madrigalists of the sixteenth and seventeenth centuries, but which instrumental composers have since Bach's day used to symbolise devilry. Such uses survived well into the twentieth century. The devil-tritone crops up in Saint-Saëns's *Danse Macabre*, in Elgar's *Dream of Gerontius*, in Stravinsky's *Soldier's Tale* and Vaughan Williams's *Job*, and in countless other works where devil's work is on hand; giving the audience, in the context, an appropriate *frisson* by reason of its associations.

Strictly speaking, there are two devils residing in the tritone. String players will stretch further for the augmented fourth and less far for the diminished fifth (the devil changes his appearance in the notation in different harmonic contexts). I think of the augmented fourth as a sharp, aggressive devil, the diminished fifth as sulky and lowering. But their characters vary with the context, and in homophonic music, the tritone-devil gets into the harmony and hides. He may contribute a restless, unstable element to the music (for instance, in the penultimate cadential chord, known to grammarians as *VIIb*); but that is the only devilish attribute left to him.

The tritone lies concealed in the harmony of the first chord of *Tristan*—a hidden symbol for *le diable au corps*, maybe? But in the music of more advanced twentieth-century composers, even the melodic tritone began to lose its devilish connotations. Schoenberg drew its sting by placing all intervals and all harmonies on an equal footing, so that it vanished from public notice as Ali Baba's house vanished when the slave-girl Morgana put a cross on all the other house-doors in the street. Bartók's favourite folk music was full of melodic tritones, so that the interval became in his hands a healthy and normal member of musical society.

If we consider the feared, disruptive influences that seem to threaten the musical state, we will find that they are treated in much the same way as feared, forbidden intervals. At first denounced, they are later gradually absorbed, domesticated, put to everyday uses. Serious musicians, after initial resistance, have come to accept the 'forbidden' techniques and instruments of popular music (and sometimes the styles and idioms as well). Recording and radio, first looked on as inventions of the devil, arch-enemies of serious music, have been accepted and assimilated, and we are beginning, after initial resistance, to allow other sorts of technological apparatus and processes into our lives.

It is easy enough to recognise the augmented-fourth devils in musical society, since they present themselves to us naked and unashamed. Pop and rock, background music, the spirit of commercialism, are loud, self-advertising devils. According to the guardians of musical morality, they steal away audiences, tempting them with seductive but worthless goods. Commerce is cynically involved in the sale of cheap music which would be dear at any price. A victory for pop is a defeat for good music.*
(Jazz, once the arch-fiend threatening the whole fabric of musical society, is now allowed to be respectable, as a sort of first cousin to serious music who prefers to live apart.)†

* A recent secretary-general of the Arts Council declared that 'Pop groups are winning the battle' as though open war had been declared. A 1977 book reviewer can only allow that 'The Beatles, *despite market pressures*, did produce several good songs.'

† 'The jazz band . . . puts itself outside the pale of music by the coarseness and vulgarity of its utterances' (W. H. Hadow, 1928). 'Jazz . . . a subject for the pathologist rather than the musician' (Arthur Bliss, 1932).

There is an element of hypocrisy and self-righteousness in many denunciations of this sort. Only a few saints and idealists are not touched by commercialism, which hides itself in the harmony of our everyday musical lives as the tritone hides itself in music. The commercial devil as rhetorically defined by many serious musicians has little more substance than the theatrical devils of Saint-Saëns's *Danse Macabre*—excellent to invoke for entertainment purposes, but that is all. (I don't mean to suggest that commercialism does not sometimes threaten serious music, but that it is often made a scapegoat for evils the musician brings on himself.)

Devils of commercialism often work in alliance with devils of bad taste. This is a group of devils of which we in England stand in particular fear. Class-consciousness, fear of being conspicuous, an often praiseworthy desire not to exaggerate or over-emphasise, and the tradition established by our earlier gentleman composers, too often lead us to ignore or suppress the commoner instincts in ourselves—which are the very instincts we should be following if we want to communicate with a world audience, throw our own minds open to world influences, and prove that music is not a refined, élitist art for connoisseurs only. Elgar, who was condemned by his academic contemporaries for loudness and vulgarity,* responded by declaring angrily that 'English music is white and avoids everything'—an accusation in which there is still a germ of truth. Brigid Brophy's more recent response to English good manners is to suggest that 'bad taste is a far more useful gift to an artist than good taste.' But in truth, we need both, just as we need our devils and our faith.

*Music must not deny its devils.* If it does so, it might just as well lie down and die at once; as so many blamelessly and perfectly composed oratorios, operas and symphonies have done in the past. In any big-scale work that aims to achieve its ends by dramatic and rhetorical means, constructional forces need to be balanced, their solidity emphasised, by the threat of destruction. So, in Shostakovich's finest symphonies, the 'black' meanings forced their way in (even when, for decorum's sake, they needed to be labelled 'anti-Soviet'); so, the Requiem needs

* 'Elgar... repugnant to many English musicians by reason of the chevalieresque rhetoric which barely covers up his basic vulgarity' (E. J. Dent).

its *Dies Irae;* musical, dramatic and theological necessities all converging. 'There must be harmonies of God in the Devil, and of the Devil in God,' Samuel Butler wrote. One of the things that disturbs me most in the present state of music is the division between high and low; which I believe to be a more serious threat to the health of the commonwealth than the fragmentation of styles and different conceptions of the aims of music found among leading contemporary composers. The high-music world does not have a monopoly of good faith, nor of sophisticated musical skills. Folk singers rise to the top of the charts not because they know how to play the market, but because they have a message for the world and their own way of putting it over. Many guitarists in the worlds of pop and rock are, in their way, as great artists as our concert-hall heroes of the keyboard and masters of flying staccato. Music should find room for conversational commonplaces as well as profound utterances, for light unguarded statements as well as for long-pondered truths. We cut ourselves off from our lower natures at our peril.

# FURTHER READING

All books referred to are listed below in the Select Bibliography.

I THE SLOPING PLAYGROUND: *Huizinga*'s views on the significance or the play-element in culture are said to be somewhat dated; but his book gives a fascinating account of the ways in which cultural games evolve and change their nature.

II THE WAY WE LIVE NOW: *Thomson*'s provocative, composer-centred account of the State of Music in the 1930s gives the reader the 'feel' of musical life in America at that time and is still relevant to our own times. *Peacock and Weir* describe the English composer's past and present economic positions, giving many facts and figures. *Roth* discusses the composer-publisher relationship and other aspects of the musical scene in post-war years from the publisher's viewpoint. *Coates*, *Jackson* and *Blades* throw light, in passing, on conditions of life in the orchestral profession over the same period. *Robinson*'s books describe the ways in which virtuoso conductors create and rule their empires. *Joel* gives the impresario's point of view, *Haendel* and *Busoni* the views of the artist who becomes, temporarily, the impresario's property. *Young*, *Farmer* and *Briggs* trace the development of subsidisation in Britain. *Arts Council*, *PEP* and *UNESCO* reports reflect the viewpoints of planners and administrators.

III MUSIC AND TECHNOLOGY: *Gaisberg* and *Gelatt* give the liveliest and most detailed accounts of the development of the recording industry. *Benjamin*'s subtle analysis of the likely effects of the technological revolution contains many interesting quotations from early essays and articles on the subject. *Chavez* discusses the coming electronic revolution as a level-headed progressive; *Russcol* considers its effects as a committed enthusiast. *Farnsworth* has some amusing examples of bizarre uses of background music; but the promotional material of the Muzak Corporation itself is the best source for the evolution and present organisation of the industry.

IV  WORLDS APART: *Hadow* and *Routley* discuss the broader issues of church music, the latter as theologian as well as musician. *Russell and Elliot*'s history of the growth of the brass band movement has much interesting information, but stops well short of the present day. *Young, Coates, Jackson* and *Blades* give between them a vivid picture of the once flourishing world of light music. *Cardew* describes the fantastic world of the extreme avant-garde of the late 1960s.

V  THE PAST THROUGH THE EARS OF THE PRESENT: *Campbell* and *Dart* describe the growth of the early-music movement and the establishment of rigorous and passionately upheld standards of work-fidelity. *Busoni*'s views on the masterpiece as the perfect, immutable work of art are reflected in many of his essays.

VI  QUESTIONS OF COMMUNICATION: *Newman* and *Slominsky* provide examples of the grand style in criticism at its best and worst. *Lee*'s long, leisurely book is a period piece, literary rather than scientific, and embodying the views of an untrained music-lover, but rewarding for those who can stay the course. *Meyer* brings great learning and perception to bear on questions of communication, and is among the more readable of musical aestheticians.

# SELECT BIBLIOGRAPHY

Place of publication is London unless otherwise indicated.

Adorno, T. W. *Introduction to the Sociology of Music* (New York: Seabury Press, 1976)
Babbitt, M. 'Who Cares If You Listen?', *High Fidelity*, February 1958
Barzun, J. *Music in American Life* (New York: Doubleday, 1956)
Benjamin, W. 'The Work of Art in the Age of Mechanical Reproduction', in *Illuminations* (Cape, 1970)
Blades, J. *Drum Roll* (Faber, 1977)
Bliss, A. 'Aspects of Contemporary Music', *Musical Times*, May 1934
Bontinck, I. *New Patterns of Musical Behaviour* (Universal, 1974)
Bornoff, J. *Music and the Twentieth Century Media*, International Music Council (Florence: 1972)
Briggs, A. *History of Broadcasting in the United Kingdom* (OUP, 1961)
Busoni, F. *Letters to his wife* (Arnold, 1938)
—— *The Essence of Music and other papers* (New York: Dover, 1965)
Campbell, D. *Dolmetsch, the man and his work* (Hamish Hamilton, 1975)
Cardew, C. *Scratch Music* (Latimer New Dimensions, 1972)
Castillejo, D. *A Counter Report on Art Patronage* (privately printed, 1968)
Chavez, C. *Towards a New Music* (1937; reprinted, New York: Norton, 1965)
Coates, E. *Suite in Four Movements* (Heinemann, 1953)
Dart, T. *Interpretation of Music* (Hutchinson, 1954)
Dent, E. J. *Ferruccio Busoni, a Biography* (1934; reprinted, Eulenberg, 1974)
Dieren, Bernard van. *Down among the dead men* (OUP, 1935)
Farmer, H. *History of the Royal Artillery Band* (RA Institution, 1954)
Farnsworth, P. *The Social Psychology of Music* (Davenport, Iowa: Iowa State Univ. Press, 1969)
Fischer, E. *Reflections on Music* (Williams and Norgate, 1951)

Foss, Hubert. *Music in My Time* (Rich and Cowan, 1933)
Gaisberg, F. *Music on Record* (Hale, 1948)
Gelatt, R. *The Fabulous Phonograph* (Cassell, 1956)
Gerhard, R. 'England, Spring 1945', *Tempo*, no. 11, 1945; reprinted in *Tempo*, no. 100, 1972
Hadow, H. *Collected Essays* (OUP, 1928)
Haendel, I. *Woman with Violin* (Gollancz, 1970)
Hindemith, P. *A Composer's World* (Cambridge, Mass: Univ. Press, Harvard 1952)
Holst, I. *Gustav Holst* (Faber, 1974)
Huizinga, J. *Homo Ludens* (Paladin, 1970)
Jackson, G. *First Flute* (Dent, 1968)
Joel, J. *I Paid the Piper* (Baker, 1970)
Keller, H. Radio 4 broadcast (*Listener*, 7 Jan. 1971)
Lambert, C. *Music Ho! A study of music in decline* (Faber [1936], 1966)
Lee, V. *Music and its Lovers* (Allen & Unwin, 1932)
Ludovici, J. Interviewed in *Good Housekeeping*, August 1965
Mawby, C. 'In Defence of Low-Fi', *Listener*, 7 Feb. 1974
Mellers, W. Review of R. Reti's *Thematic Process in Music*, *Music and Letters*, xxxiv, no. 2, 1953
Menuhin, Y. *Unfinished Journey* (Macdonald & Jane's, 1976)
Meyer, L. B. *Music, the Arts and Ideas* (Chicago, Ill.: Univ. of Chicago Press, 1967)
Miller, J. 'Jonathan Miller talks to Max Loppert', *Music & Musicians*, April 1974
Newman, E. *Essays from the World of Music* (Calder, 1956)
Peacock, A. and Weir, R. *The Composer in the Market Place* (Faber, 1975)
Pearsall, R. *Edwardian Popular Music* (David & Charles, 1975)
Pegge, R. Morley 'The Horn, and the Later Brass' in *Musical Instruments Through the Ages*, ed. Anthony Baines (Pelican, 1961)
Plaistow, S. 'Society and the Composer', *Composer*, Summer 1972
Political and Economic Planning. *Sponsorship of Music: the role of local authorities* (1966)
Robinson, P. *Karajan* (Macdonald & Jane's, 1976)
—— *Stokowski* (Macdonald & Jane's, 1977)
Roth, E. *The Business of Music* (Cassell, 1969)
Routh, F. *The Patronage and Presentation of Contemporary Music* (Redcliffe Concerts, 1970)

Routley, E. *Words, Music and the Church* (Jenkins, 1969)
Rump, A. *Money for Composers* (Arts Council, 1977)
Russcol, H. and Banai, M. *Philharmonic: A great symphony orchestra—its men, its women, its passions* (New English Library, 1972)
Russell, J. and Elliot, J. H. *The Brass Band Movement* (Dent, 1936)
Russell, T. A. 'Conductorless Orchestras', *Musical Times*, May 1938
Schoenberg, A. *Letters* (Faber, 1964)
Seashore, C. *The Psychology of Musical Talent* (Boston: Silver, Burdett Co. 1919)
Slominsky, N. *Lexicon of Musical Invective* (Seattle, Wash.: Univ. of Washington Press, 1953)
Smith Brindle, R. 'Notes from Abroad', *Musical Times*, November 1955
Stravinsky, I. *Stravinsky in Conversation with Robert Craft* (Faber, 1959)
Stravinsky, I. and Craft, R. *Dialogues and a Diary* (Faber, 1968)
—— *Themes and Conclusions* (Faber, 1972)
Taylor, R. *The Fifth Estate: Britain's Unions in the 1970s* (Routledge & Kegan Paul, 1978)
Thomson, V. *The State of Music*, 2nd edn. rev. (New York: Vintage Books, 1962)
UNESCO. 'Music and Technology', *Revue Musicale* (Paris), 1971
Young, K. *Music's Great Days in the Spas and Watering Places* (Macmillan, 1968)
Westrup, J. A. 'Bandsmen's Huts and Suburban Vestries', *Musical Times*, April 1961
White, D. 'What is a Luxury?', *New Society*, 23 Sept. 1975

# INDEX

*Akenfield* (Ronald Blythe), 35
Albert (Prince Consort), 54
*Alceste* (Gluck), 33
aleatoric music, 75; relationship with light music, 104
*Alice through the Looking Glass* (Lewis Carroll), 10
Alkan, C. H., 79
amateurs, 28, 29–34; bands and choirs, 32; conductors, 31; conservatism of, 34; early music and, 113; professionals' opinion of, 31
analysis and theory, 130–2
archetypes, 20–3
army bands, 50, 51, 54, 57
Arnold, Malcolm, 34, 103
Arts Associations, 28, 55-6, 105
Arts Council of Great Britain, 47, 48, 53, 55, 146n
Auxetophone, 83
authenticity, 113–18; commercialism and, 116; critics' views on, 129; in early music, 112; music-drama and, 117; organists limited by, 94; university musicians and, 117
avant-garde, 104–9, 110, 124

BBC, 38, 47, 48, 52, 56n; light music division, 103; salon orchestra, 102; staff orchestras, 36; Symphony Orchestra, 35
Babbitt, Milton, 82, 125, 132, 133
Bach, Johann Sebastian, 24, 68, 105, 130, 139; Brandenburg Concertos, 77, 110; Passions, 114; B minor Mass, 130; choral preludes, 130
background music, 84–8
Bailleux (publisher), 48
Baillot (philosopher), 140
Banai, Margalit, 20

Barnes, Clive, 127
Bartók, Bela, 28, 121, 138, 146
Barzun, Jacques, 125
Bath, 50; spa orchestra, 50n
Bax, Arnold, 79
Beard, Paul, 50n
Beatles, the, 146n
Beecham, Thomas, 38, 50n, 64, 114
Beethoven, Ludwig van, 10, 18, 20, 22, 24, 42, 71, 74, 87, 89, 103, 105, 107, 115, 116, 117, 119, 120, 121, 130, 134, 136, 140; Archduke Trio, 136; *Egmont* Overture, 17, 136; Fifth Symphony, 33, 62, 63, 119, 130, 136, 140; Sixth Symphony, 115; Ninth Symphony (Choral), 72, 118; 'Battle' Symphony, 73, 74
Beeton, Mrs, 117
Benjamin, Walter, 141
Bennett, Richard Rodney, 144n
Berg, Alban, 138; *Wozzeck*, 82, 136
Berio, Luciano, 83, 89, 126, 128
Berlin Philharmonic Orchestra, 49, 53, 62
Berlioz, Hector, 78, 95, 97, 121
Bernstein, Leonard, 21
Birtwistle, Harrison, 34, 100
Blaukopf, Kurt, 73
Bliss, Arthur, 24, 146n
*Bohème, La* (Puccini), 30
*Bohème, Scènes de la vie de* (Mürger), 20
Boosey and Hawkes, 56n
*Boris Godunov* (Moussorgsky), 114
Boulez, Pierre, 33, 34, 37, 42, 72, 125, 132, 133, 138, 142, 144
Bourgeois, Derek, 100
Bournemouth, municipal council, 53; Symphony Orchestra, 35
Brahms, Johannes, 24, 63, 78, 87, 107, 114

Brain, Aubrey, 35
brass bands, 95, 96–100
Brendel, Alfred, 21
Brian, Havergal, 79
Bridge, Frank, 101
*British Bandsman, The*, 97, 99
*British Mouthpiece, The*, 97
Britten, Benjamin, 34, 56n, 77, 121, 128; Second Quartet, 131
Brophy, Brigid, 147
Bruckner, Anton: Seventh Symphony, 129
Bruggen, Franz, 111
Buffet bassoon, 115
Burney, Charles, 84
Busoni, Ferruccio, 23, 28, 32, 40, 47, 80, 120, 123, 127
Butler, Samuel, 133, 148
Buxtehude, Diderik, 136
Byrd, William, 91

Caballé, Monserrat, 119
Caerphilly cheese, 79n
Cage, John, 106, 107, 126
Camden, Archie, 35
Canterbury, Archbishop of, 54
Cardew, Cornelius, 142; *Treatise*, 143n
Cardus, Neville, 128
Carlyle, Thomas, 24
Carter, Elliott, 125, 138
Cary, Tristram, 81
*Cassell's Magazine*, 66
Castillejo, David: *Counter Report on Art Patronage*, 55n
Catgut Acoustical Society of America, 60
Chavez, Carlos, 75, 80
*Chu Chin Chow* (Norton), 32
China, scales in ancient, 131
Chopin, Frédéric: First Prelude, 31
church music, 90–6
cinema: *see* organists, cinema
Clark, Kenneth, 78
Cleveland Quartet, 140n
Cockney rhyming slang, 123
commercialism, 9, 47–8, 56, 117, 121, 143, 146, 147
communication problems, 122–5
competitions, 17, 98–9

composers, 23–9; attitude to masterworks, 120–1; attitude to money, 23–4; church music and, 95–6; communication problems of, 122–4; mechanical media and, 75–6; performers and, 26–7, 142–3; performer-composers, 107; programme notes by, 131–2; status, 25–7
Composers' Guild of Great Britain, 23; Composers' Guilds, 26
Conan Doyle, Arthur, 66
conductorless ensembles, 45
conductors, 31, 38, 42–6
Connolly, Cyril, 89
*Constant Nymph, The* (Margaret Kennedy), 20
Contemporary Music Network, 53
Copland, Aaron, 82, 103, 124
*Coq d'Or* (Rimsky-Korsakov), 35
Council for the Encouragement of Music and the Arts (CEMA), 52, 53
Covent Garden (Opera House), 44, 114n
Cowell, Henry, 106
critics, 127–30
Crumb, George, 83; *Black Angels*, 131

Day, Alfred, 130
Debussy, Claude, 78
Delius, Frederic, 78
*Dies Irae*, 148
Dolmetsch, Arnold, 112
Domingo, Placido, 119
Don Quixote, 65
Donizetti, Gaetano, 79
Dykes, J. B., 91

early music, 17, 110–13; *Early Music* (periodical), 111
Eastman School Orchestra, 33
Edison, Thomas A., 62; Edison-Bell Company, 66
electronic music, 80–3
Elgar, Edward, 22, 62, 63, 98, 101, 102, 124, 129, 142, 147; *Cockaigne* overture, 63; *Dream of Gerontius*, 145; First Symphony, 114; Violin Concerto, 63; light-music clichés in, 102

# INDEX

Eliot, George, 20
English musicians, their characteristics, 21–2, 24, 147
Entertainments National Service Association (ENSA), 52
entrepreneurs, 46–9
Equity (actors' union), 34

Feldman, Morton, 106, 142, 144
Fenby, Eric, 50n
Field, John, 79
Fischer, Edwin, 116
Fletcher, Percy, 97, 100; *Labour and Love*, 97
Ford Foundation for Suppression of Unpromising Composers, 57
Foss, Hubert, 27
Franck, César, 78
Frazer, Sir J. G., 92
functional music, 89, 90

Gaisberg, Fred, 44n, 61n
game-elements in music, 14–19, 124
gambling and betting industries, 36
Gavle (Sweden), 53
Geehl, Henry, 97
Gerhard, Roberto, 34, 98, 134
German, Edward, 103
Globokar, Vinco, 107
Glock, William, 56n
Glyndebourne, 44
Goossens, Eugene, 101
Goossens, Leon, 102
Gounod, Charles, 'Lend me your Aid' (*Queen of Sheba*), 97–8
Grainger, Percy, 80
gramophone: *see* mechanical media; recording
Greater London Council, 53
'Gregorian Chant, Popular Hits of', 111
Grillparzer, Franz, 133
Grimethorpe, Lord, 117
Grove's *Dictionary of Music*, 97
Guy, Barry, 107

Hadow, W. H., 91, 146n
Haitink, Bernard, 21, 58
Handel, George Frederick: Concerti Grossi, 116; oratorios and *Water Music*, 114

Hanslick, Eduard, 127
Harty, Hamilton, 114
Haydn, Joseph, 33, 48, 103, 116, 119, 120, 134, 141, 142; piano trios, 114; Quartet in F, op. 3, no. 5, 48
Hazlitt, William, 24
Heinichen, Johann: *Der Generalbass in der Composition*, 145
Henze, Hans Werner, 21
Heykens, Jon, 103
hifi: *see* recording
Hindemith, Paul, 43, 129, 137; *A Composer's World*, 137
Hoffstetter, R., 48
Holliger, Heinz, 107
Holmes, Sherlock, 66
Holst, Gustav, 39, 96, 103
Honegger, Arthur, 80
Hopi Indians, 94
Hotteterre, Jacques, 79
Huizinga, J., 17
Hume, Ord, 97
Hummel, Nepomuk, 79
Huxley, Aldous, 20
Hylton, Jack, 40n

impresarios: *see* entrepreneurs
Ives, Charles, 57, 79, 106

Jagger, Mick, 21
James, William, 139
jazz, 53, 72, 146
Jenkins, Cyril, 100
*Journal of Music Theory*, 131

Kabalevsky, Dmitri, 77
Kagel, Mauricio, 106, 107, 126; 'Two Man Band', 107
Karajan, Herbert von, 67
Kell, Reginald, 102
Keller, Hans, 38
King's College Chapel, Cambridge, 91
Kreisler, Fritz, 63

Lamoureux, Charles, 51
Lalandi, Lina, 56n
Lambert, Constant, 77
Langdon, J. N., 86
Lassus, Orlando, 89, 91

Lee, Vernon, 135, 137, 139; *Music and its Lovers*, 135
Legge, Walter, 64
Leyland, British, 58
Ligeti, György, 89
light music, 101–4
'Lili Marlene', 17n
Link Aviation Trainer, 60
listening processes, 76–9, 133–41; co-constructive, 137; distracted listening, 141; effects of radio and recording on, 76–9; intuitive listening, 138; questionnaires on, 135
Liszt, Franz, 20, 78, 98, 134, 135
London County Council, 51
London Philharmonic Orchestra (LPO), 35
London Symphony Orchestra (LSO), 33, 53
long-playing records: see mechanical media; recording
Ludovici, John, 141
'Lunatic Fringe, The', 81
'luxuries, essential', 58

Macallum, David, 50n
Machaut, Guillaume de, 72
Maclean, Alick, 50n
McLuhan, Herbert Marshall, 89, 125
Mahler, Gustav, 20, 58, 69, 73, 78, 89, 114; *Song of the Earth*, 74
'Marseillaise, La', 17n
Mawby, Colin, 67
mechanical media, 61–88; composers and, 75, 76; idea of fidelity, 65–70; listeners and, 76–9; orchestras depend on, 64–5; performers and, 72–3; publishers and, 48; record better than real thing, 69; traditions, lack of, 61
Mellers, Wilfred, 97, 120, 130–1
Mendelssohn, Felix, 125
Menuhin, Yehudi, 68, 71, 89n
Messiaen, Olivier, 56n
Meyer, Leonard, 143
Milhaud, Darius, 75
Miller, Jonathan, 118
Milton, John, 24
Modupe, Prince, 138

Moog-synthesised Bach, 68, 83
Moozak (horse), 85
Morgan, William de, 20
Morley Pegge, R., 98
Mozart, Wolfgang Amadeus, 22, 50n, 107, 114, 116, 118, 120, 121, 125; *In diesen heil'gen Hallen*, 115; Symphony in G minor, 118; *Voi che sapete*, 98
municipal music, 50, 51
Munrow, David, 111
*Musical Times, The*, 81, 97
Musicians' Union, 36, 84
Muzak, 85–6

National Youth Brass Band, 53; National Youth Orchestra, 33, 53, 72
*New Statesman and Nation*, 128
*New York Times*, 127
Newman, Ernest, 70n, 127, 136
Nielsen, Carl, 124
Nikisch, Artur, 62, 66
notation: graphical, 107; as 'engine of immortality', 108

Old Vic, The, 114
orchestral players, 34–9; see also performers
organists, 33, 39, 92–4; cinema, 94
Ormandy, Eugene, 43

Palestrina, Giovanni, 145
Palm, Siegfried, 107
panatrope, 34
Papuan headhunters, 96
Parry, Hubert, 24
Patti, Adelina, 62, 66
performers (professional), 29–32; conductors and, 43; security of, 57; standards influenced by recording, 72–3
Performing Right Society, 23, 48
*Persimfans* (conductorless orchestra), 45n
Philadelphia Orchestra, 43
Philharmonia Orchestra, 64
Philharmonic Society of London, 51
phonograph: see mechanical media; recording
Pini, Anthony, 102

## INDEX

Pilgrim Trust, 53
Pioch, George, 78n
Plaistow, Stephen, 55
player piano (pianola), 63, 64
Portsmouth Sinfonia, 143n
Powell, Anthony, 20
Powell, Claude, 47
*Prince Igor* dances (Borodin), 50n
professionalism, 17–18, 29–31; *see also* performers
programme notes, 131–2
Proust, Marcel, 64
Prout, Ebenezer, 114
publishers, 48, 107
Puccini, Giacomo, 63

Quantz, Johann, 79
quota systems, 55

Rachmaninov, Serge, 71, 142
radio, 61, 63, 72, 73, 75, 76–9; *see also* BBC; mechanical media
Ray, Cyril, 127
Raynor, Henry, 102n
recording, 61–79; *see also* mechanical media
Reed, Henry: *Hilda Tablet*, 81
Reich, Steve, 87, 107, 108
Reich, Willi, 143
Reimann, Karl, 130, 131
Reinganum (cartoonist), 84
Reti, Rudolf, 130, 131
Richter, Hans, 115
Riddle, Frederick, 102
Riley, Terry, 108
Rimmer (brass band arranger), 97
*Robert le Diable* (Meyerbeer), 134
Robin Hood, 14
Ronald, Landon, 62
Rossini, Gioacchino: *William Tell Overture*, 143n
Rostropovich, Mstislav, 71
Roth, Ernst, 26, 114n
Royal Artillery Orchestra, 51
Royal College of Organists, 93n
Runciman, John, 115
Russcol, Herbert, 20, 82

Saint-Saëns, Camille: *Danse Macabre*, 145, 147
Saki (H. H. Munro), 43
Salvation Army, 91, 95

Salzman, Eric, 143
Satie, Erik, 106
Scarborough (spa and orchestra), 50, 51
Scarlatti, Domenico, 115
Schenker, Heinrich, 130
Schoenberg, Arnold, 23, 28, 95, 115, 123, 125, 127, 128, 135, 140, 142; Orchestral Variations, 67; *Pierrot Lunaire*, 72, 82
Schubert, Franz, 22; *An die Musik*, 98
Schwarzkopf, Elisabeth, 121
Schweitzer, Albert, 130
Scott, Cyril, 101
Seashore, Carl, 137
Shakespeare, William, 24
Shaw, George Bernard, 35
Shostakovich, Dmitri, 16, 121, 147
Sibelius, Jean, 124, 129, 142
Simpson, Robert, 124, 129
*skalds*, Icelandic, 123
Smith Brindle, Reginald, 81
Smyth, Ethel, 17
soloists, 39–42
Solti, Georg, 21
Stainer, John: *The Crucifixion*, 96
Stockhausen, Karlheinz, 21, 82, 106, 107, 121, 126, 142; *Gesang der Jünglinge*, 81; *Hymnen*, 79; *Mikrophonie II*, 82
Stokowski, Leopold, 67
Strauss, Richard, 24, 89, 98, 128; *Ein Heldenleben*, 115; *Till Eulenspiegel*, 78
Stravinsky, Igor, 24, 28, 42, 57, 75, 86, 95, 121, 124, 126, 129, 135, 136; *The Flood*, 33; Octet, 115; *Oedipus Rex*, 33; *Rite of Spring*, 33, 72, 78n; *The Soldier's Tale*, 136, 145
Stroh violin, 63
subsidy, 50–9; army bands, 51, 54, 57; BBC, 52; commercial, 56; municipal, 50–2; state, 49, 52–7
Sullivan, Arthur, 22

Tallis, Thomas, 92
Tchaikovsky, Peter Ilyich, 74, 98, 118; *1812* Overture, 74; Violin Concerto, 134

Telemann, G. P., 110
Thomson, Virgil, 24, 136, 139
*Times, The*, 50
Tortelier, Paul, 21
*Tosca* (Puccini), 47
Tovey, Donald Francis, 16, 114, 127
tritone, 145–6
'Trumpeters Wild', 100

under-cranking, 123
U.S. Army Human Engineering Department, 86
universities: analysis and theory at, 131; early music movement in, 41; intellectuals and visionaries at, 105; musicological know-how, 111; orchestral players from, 36; scholarly morality and, 117
Urban (linguist), 10

van Dieren, Bernard, 32
Varèse, Edgard, 28, 123
Vaughan Williams, Ralph, 24, 96, 129; *Job*, 145
Verdi, Giuseppe, 119
Verne, Jules, 80
Vienna Philharmonic Orchestra, 49
Vivaldi, Antonio, 77, 89, 142

Wagner, Richard, 20, 22, 29, 63, 77, 95, 98, 114, 115, 118, 128, 136; *Meistersinger* overture, 51; *The Ring*, 23; *Tannhäuser* overture, 115; *Tristan*, 114, 130, *Liebestod* from, 85
Walter, Bruno, 64
Walton, William, 124
Weingartner, Felix, 63, 118
Wells, H. G., 121
Westrup, J. A., 98
White, David, 58
Whorf, Benjamin Lee, 94
Wieniawski, Henryk, 112
Wishart, Peter, 129
Wolf, Hugo, 22
Wood, Haydn, 103
Wood, Henry, 38
Wyatt, S., 86

$x$-factors, in live performance, 70, 71; in early music, 112
Xenakis, Iannides, 56n, 130

$y$-factors, in recorded music, 71

Zavertal, Ladislav, 51